NEW YORK CITY IN THE GREAT DEPRESSION

SHELTERING THE HOMELESS

On the cover: Please see page 44. (Author's collection.)

NEW YORK CITY IN THE GREAT DEPRESSION
SHELTERING THE HOMELESS

Dorothy Laager Miller

ARCADIA
PUBLISHING

ISBN 978-0-7385-6597-2

Published by Arcadia Publishing
Charleston SC, Chicago IL, Portsmouth NH, San Francisco CA

Printed in the United States of America

Library of Congress Control Number: 2009922372

For all general information contact Arcadia Publishing at:
Telephone 843-853-2070
Fax 843-853-0044
E-mail sales@arcadiapublishing.com
For customer service and orders:
Toll-Free 1-888-313-2665

Visit us on the Internet at www.arcadiapublishing.com

Dedicated to my children so they will know what a great man their great-grandfather was. I hope it shows them that you do not judge a successful life by the amount of possessions you have but by the number of your fellow men you have helped.

Contents

ACKNOWLEDGMENTS

Many people have contributed to the development of this book. Unless otherwise noted, all images appear courtesy of the author's collection. I am indebted foremost to Adelaide Mendyka, daughter of the superintendent of the Municipal Lodging House, for her interpretation of the photographs. I owe a considerable debt to Jo Ann Laager for her computer skills and knowledge. Thanks to William Gaias for his enthusiasm and support, which I always depend on. I also wish to thank Mildred Mastrion for her photographs of her immigrant ancestors. Thanks also go to Helen Collins, my aunt, for her contribution of photographs and her knowledge of the Depression time period. Many thanks go to David Favaloro, director of curatorial affairs for the Lower East Side Tenement Museum, for his historical knowledge of the time period. Finally and most importantly, I thank my friend Paul Infranco and my husband, William Miller, two local historians, for their encouragement and historical knowledge.

INTRODUCTION

I first became interested in the topic of the Great Depression when I found my grandfather's scrapbook and collection of photographs in the cellar of my mother's house. The scrapbook contained the newspaper clippings from 1929 to 1955 that pertained to my grandfather's work and the Municipal Lodging House. My grandfather Joseph A. Mannix, superintendent of the Municipal Lodging House, used the scrapbook as his journal of his work. This book is a pictorial history of the shelters provided by New York City for the homeless during the Great Depression. It begins with the stock market crash of 1929, discussing the Municipal Lodging House and its annexes in Manhattan, the farm colony at Camp LaGuardia, and the rehabilitation center at Hart Island. It shows the famous Depression breadlines, Mayor Jimmy Walker, Gov. Al Smith, many landscapes of New York City, immigrants, tenement housing, and the political machine of Tammany Hall.

The photographs in this book give the flavor of the 1930s and 1940s. They show the hardships that many New Yorkers as well as all Americans encountered during the Great Depression. The photographs show the despair in the faces of the homeless and hungry. This is a pictorial salute to the perseverance of New Yorkers during the longest period of unemployment activity in modern times. It recounts many riches-to-rags stories, showing that no one was exempt from the hard times. Millions of Americans suffered from malnutrition. People could not pay their mortgages so they lost their homes. They had to roam the country looking for food, shelter, and a job. Luckily, the City of New York came to their rescue, providing them with temporary food and shelter at the Municipal Lodging House and its annexes. Later the city tried an experiment at Camp LaGuardia to provide a more stable and permanent environment for the homeless of New York City.

When faced with the monumental problem of feeding and sheltering the homeless in New York City, the welfare department and its administrators rose to the occasion and helped the unfortunate people of the city. The welfare department provided an organized and immediate response to this major problem. The department prevented widespread starvation until Franklin D. Roosevelt was elected president. Roosevelt provided a wide variety of federally funded programs to try to restore the American economy. It was only when Roosevelt drafted six million soldiers and six million defense workers for World War II that the Great Depression came to an end.

This history will show in detail the facilities and programs offered by the welfare department for the homeless people of New York City. The photographs in this book are unique. Some of the outstanding images in this book include inimitable detailed pictures of the interiors of the Municipal Lodging House and its annexes and copies of letters of appreciation sent to the superintendent from foreign dignitaries and the lodgers themselves.

According to the records of the superintendent of the Municipal Lodging House, Joseph A. Mannix, in the year 1932, about 4,300 homeless men showed up for free lodgings and for their morning and evening meals each day of the year whether it was summer or winter. Men were supposed to apply for their night's lodging at the Central Registration Bureau at South Ferry. However, a homeless person was not refused admission to the Municipal Lodging House because he had not adhered to this rule. When people did apply directly to the Municipal Lodging House for food or shelter without going first to the Central Registration Bureau, they were given a night's lodging and food, but they were directed to go to the Central Registration Bureau for the homeless the next day to register. This bureau was opened on October 1, 1931, and was located at the foot of Whitehall Street in the borough of Manhattan. The Central Registration Bureau received cooperation from local agencies including the Municipal Lodging House, which cared for the homeless people. At this bureau, the homeless were registered and given an identification card to be used when applying for admission to the shelter to which they were assigned. If individuals were assigned to the Municipal Lodging House, they would go directly to the Municipal Lodging House building at East 25th Street. They were given food and shelter there on that night. On subsequent nights, they were assigned to either of the two annexes. These homeless persons were not required to reregister unless for some reason, best known to them, they might stay away from the lodging house. If they did this, then they were required to reregister at the Central Registration Bureau.

As told by Joseph A. Mannix, superintendent of the Municipal Lodging House, in his journal, let us follow a homeless man through the procedure at the Municipal Lodging House. The man's history, if he was applying for the first time, was taken as soon as he arrived. No unnecessary data was asked for or required. He was asked his name, age, birthplace, number of years in the United States and New York City, last address he called home, last place he was employed, his normal occupation, war service, if any, whether married or single, and the name of a relative or friend to be notified in case of an emergency. The lodger was then given a pair of brass checks of identical numbers and was shown to the dining room where the supper menu consisted of a well-balanced meal. After their supper, the lodger was shown to the disrobing room where he would disrobe, hang up all his clothes, and fasten one of the brass checks to the clothing. All clothes were immediately placed in specially built heat chambers and sterilized by dry heat during the night. Meanwhile, the lodger was given a towel and a nightshirt. After taking a shower, he proceeded to the physician for a medical examination. After that, he went to the sleeping quarters. The sleeping facilities consisted of double-decked iron beds, a folded blanket instead of a mattress (for hygiene purposes), a blanket covering, clean sheets, and pillowcases. Both the heating and ventilating systems of the sleeping quarters were well regulated. Sleeping quarters were kept constantly clean. In the morning, the lodgers were free to go where they pleased with the exception of a certain number of men who assisted in cleaning and making up the beds. These men were given a noonday meal. This noonday meal was in addition to the breakfast all lodgers received.

Women lodgers had their own living quarters, the second and third floors of the lodging house proper. They also had their own dining room. They had a sitting room with a piano and a radio. The women were provided a sewing machine for their use and a laundry room where they could wash their own clothes if they wanted to.

According to Joseph A. Mannix's journal, a total of 889,000 night lodgings for men, women, and children were given during the year 1931. The year 1932 showed a tremendous increase of 462,000 lodgers. There was a considerable amount of social work carried on at the Municipal Lodging House. In this connection, the Municipal Lodging House cooperated with the various other bureaus of the New York City Department of Welfare. To this end, many lodgers beyond the age of 70 years were given old-age relief pensions, poor were returned to their places of legal settlement, and alien and nonresident poor were held awaiting deportation. Food and lodging was furnished to those awaiting admission to the New York City home by the department of hospitals. Assistance was rendered to lodgers in connection with claims pending with the state department of labor. Many boys and young men were placed in other agencies where contact with the more hardened adult type was eliminated. Veterans were assisted by being referred to the appropriate organizations for necessary aid in obtaining hospitalization and other benefits. Aid was obtained for lodgers from relatives in other cities and countries. Lodgers whose children or other relatives were found to be capable of assisting with their support were referred to family court for necessary action. Special arrangements were made to provide food and lodging for a number of homeless persons receiving clinical and convalescent care at Bellevue Hospital. Many persons in need of care were sent to various hospitals in the city for proper treatment. In the cases of the young girls who applied to the Municipal Lodging House, those who were under the age of 21 were referred to the Crime Prevention Bureau for such deposition as was necessary.

In the spring of 1934, on a farm situated on the uplands of Orange County, 65 miles north of New York City, a pioneer venture in rehabilitation took place. This farm was known as Camp Greycourt. The farm was started by the New York City Department of Welfare to care for the men of the Municipal Lodging House. It started as a farm colony for unemployed men during the Depression. Progressive thinkers thought that a country setting was just the thing for discouraged and demoralized city dwellers. The unemployed needed not only food and shelter but a purpose in life. The farm at Greycourt gave them a purpose—it gave them a job. The camp was over 300 acres. The facility was built in 1918 and first served as a correctional facility for women until 1934 when it was turned over to the welfare department. The camp was renamed Camp LaGuardia in 1935 after New York City's exuberant mayor Fiorello LaGuardia. The reason for the camp was to provide temporary relief for the unemployed and homeless people in New York City. The camp included a 191-acre farm that provided food for the residents, and 150 residents worked on the farm. In the camp's early years, the residents found work at the large Catskill resorts. Every day a bus would pick up the homeless and jobless from the streets of New York City and drive them 65 miles outside the city to Camp LaGuardia.

The 73-year-old camp closed in 2007. Mayor Michael Bloomberg said the city wanted to get away from temporary shelters and move more toward subsidized housing. Local opposition was also involved in its closing. Many local people complained about the residents of the camp wandering into town drunk and urinating in public. Before closing, the camp had a budget of $19 million. The city wants to spend this money on longer-term solutions such as subsidized housing with social services.

Hart Island, sometimes referred to as Hart's Island, is a small island in the Long Island Sound. It is a mile long and a quarter mile wide. It consists of 131 acres and is the easternmost part of the Bronx. The island was bought from the Native Americans by Thomas Pell in the 1600s. Hart Island has been used as a workhouse, a hospital, a Civil War internment camp, a rehabilitation camp for homeless men, a Nike missile base, and a potter's field for the City of New York. The New York City Board of Estimates agreed that the island be used as a rehabilitation home for 2,000 men in 1950. Joseph A. Mannix was the director of Hart Island at that time.

The department of correction took control of the island in 1954, and it was used for those committing minor offences. The prison closed in 1966, and the office of narcotics administration utilized Hart Island as a rehabilitation center for drug addicts. It created Phoenix House there, and it thrived until 1976 when the high cost of operating the ferry caused it to close.

Hopefully this pictorial history of the Depression in New York City will help to illustrate how the welfare department of this great city dealt with one of the darkest times in recent history. In our present time of economic unrest, this topic is again at the forefront of the American people's minds. People may be interested in reading about the circumstances that brought the Great Depression to our country. They will be able to look at the exclusive photographs that depict how New Yorkers dealt with the problem. They will be able to see firsthand the faces of New York citizens dealing with poverty, unemployment, and homelessness.

One

Municipal Lodging House and Annexes

The stock market crash of October 1929 was the prelude to the Great Depression. It was a time of hardship and sorrow for Americans. Money, shelter, food, and jobs were scarce. Due to the bad economy, New Yorkers were forced to wander the streets for food and shelter. The New York City Department of Welfare and its city administrators rose to the occasion and helped the unfortunate citizens of New York City. The welfare department provided an organized and immediate response to the overwhelming needs of the poor. The department prevented widespread starvation until Franklin D. Roosevelt was elected president.

The Municipal Lodging House and its two annexes were operated under the supervision of the New York City Department of Welfare, of which Frank Taylor was the commissioner during the Great Depression. It was the city's shelter for men, women, and children and operated in accordance with section 5, chapter 535 of the laws of 1886. The first Municipal Lodging House opened on December 2, 1896, and was located at First Avenue and 23rd Street in Manhattan. This institution was in operation until the latter part of 1909. The new Municipal Lodging House was erected in 1908 and opened in 1909. It was located at 432 East 25th Street in Manhattan.

During the late 1920s and early 1930s, continued unemployment and widespread depression made it necessary for the City of New York to provide more commodious quarters for the homeless. As a result, the New York City Department of Welfare provided two annexes to the original main lodging house. Annex No. 1 was on city pier No. 73 at the front of East 25th Street. Annex No. 2 was in the Manhattan terminal building of the old 39th Street Brooklyn ferry at the front of Whitehall Street, South Ferry. The bed capacity of the Municipal Lodging House proper for men, women, and children was 910. That of Annex No. 1 was 3,000, and Annex No. 2 was 1,946. Both annexes housed men only. Thus, the total number of free beds furnished each night by the City of New York for the homeless, the unemployed, and other unfortunates was 5,856 beds.

Supt. Joseph A. Mannix had a monumental job to perform. He had to coordinate several agencies depending on the problems that arose. He was a great humanitarian at a time when New York City needed one.

Pictured here in 1914 is the manufacturing room of the original Municipal Lodging House. All who were able were assigned to the industrial department where they would join a trade gang, a shop, or an unskilled worker's gang. This enabled them to work their way back to independence. This was at a time when New York's homeless and jobless were at a minimum and, therefore, people were offered many more services.

In 1910, when this picture of the Municipal Lodging House was taken, the facility was run by the department of public charities. Pictured here is the reception room of the lodging house. The number of applicants was relatively small in comparison to the numbers in the Depression years.

The pier at the front of East 25th Street is pictured in 1914. This pier was later used as Annex No. 1 of the Municipal Lodging House in 1930. This pier was later called the "largest bedroom in the world" by the "Ripley's Believe It or Not!" newspaper column.

The welfare office for dependent children in the old Municipal Lodging House is shown around 1914. The first Municipal Lodging House opened on December 2, 1896, and was located at First Avenue and 23rd Street in the borough of Manhattan.

Pictured in September 1937 is the Municipal Lodging House on East 25th Street in New York City. Partially shown on the left is pier No. 73, used for the overflow from the shelter at the Municipal Lodging House run by the welfare department of New York City. On the lower right side of the picture, unemployed men line up for food and shelter. Notice the USA Work sign. This was the largest New Deal agency. The Works Progress Administration (WPA) employed millions of people in the United States during the Great Depression. The goal of the WPA was to employ most of the unemployed people on relief until the economy improved. (New-York Historical Society.)

Joseph A. Mannix, superintendent of the Municipal Lodging House, and Frank Taylor (right), commissioner of the welfare department in New York City, are shown around 1930 standing in front of the Municipal Lodging House.

Shown in this picture are the breadlines outside the Municipal Lodging House on December 25, 1931. The noonday meal is being served. The Municipal Lodging House was located on East 25th Street. Looking west are First, Second, and Third Avenues. On the south side, in the foreground, is the New York water supply. The six-story building is the Municipal Lodging House.

East 25th Street is shown as it appears today. More than 80 years ago, the Municipal Lodging House stood where the VA medical center now stands. Today the street is lined with cars. During the time of the Great Depression, the street was lined with starving, homeless men waiting patiently for admittance into the Municipal Lodging House for food and a warm bed.

Pictured in 1930 are the children of Supt. Joseph A. Mannix and the children of other employees of the Municipal Lodging House and friendly police officer Sokco. The children played on East 25th Street in front of the Municipal Lodging House proper.

Shown here are, from left to right, the children of Joseph A. Mannix: Annamae, Adelaide, and Dorothy Mannix. The girls are riding their bicycles on the sidewalk in front of the Municipal Lodging House on East 25th Street.

The breadlines of New York City during the Great Depression are captured in this c. 1930 photograph. The men are lined up on East 25th Street waiting to eat and be admitted to the Municipal Lodging House for shelter. These men are very orderly and peaceful despite being hungry and homeless.

This tray of stew, coffee, and other food was given to this woman, Jean, at the Municipal Lodging House on December 10, 1932. It was so tempting that she lost all sense of etiquette by completely forgetting the existence of forks, knives, and spoons. "Your stew is real good," she explained to Supt. Joseph A. Mannix.

The noonday meal line is pictured on Sunday, May 10, 1931. Homeless and jobless, the unfortunate men of New York City patiently wait for their lunches at the Municipal Lodging House on East 25th Street. The men are 10 deep stretching down East 25th Street.

The back entrance to the Municipal Lodging House, pictured here around 1930, is on the left near where the policeman is standing. The nurse's home of Bellevue Hospital is across the street (the dark building), and next door to that are tenement buildings.

The storage room for the lodgers' clothes, which were fumigated during the night, and the fumigating room at the Municipal Lodging House are shown in this c. 1930 photograph. The men pictured were two of the many who clamored to work for their food and lodging rather than to accept a handout.

The stock market crash of October 1929 was the prelude to the Great Depression. It was a time of hardship and sorrow for Americans. Money, shelter, and food were scarce. Because of the scarcity of money, Americans could not pay their rent. They were forced to wander the streets searching for shelter. This January 4, 1931, photograph depicts the homeless and hungry waiting to be admitted to the Municipal Lodging House, located at 432 East 25th Street in New York City, for the noonday meal.

The noonday meal line is shown on May 10, 1931. The homeless wait for their lunches at the Municipal Lodging House.

A delivery of meat arrives at the Municipal Lodging House around 1930. The meat is examined by an assistant to Supt. Joseph A. Mannix. The lodging house served lamb or beef stew daily. It required enough meat to serve thousands of people.

Above is the food storage room at the Municipal Lodging House around 1930. To feed thousands of people daily, the city had on hand crates of fresh fruits and vegetables, such as peaches, bags of potatoes, and onions. The city had a monumental task taking care of the homeless and the starving during the Great Depression.

The meat locker of the Municipal Lodging House during the Great Depression was always filled to capacity, as seen here around 1930. At this time, the City of New York fed thousands of homeless, starving people. The lodging house made beef or lamb stew to feed its residents.

Cooks prepare Christmas dinner for the lodgers at the Municipal Lodging House. For Christmas 1930, the Municipal Lodging House made one of the biggest efforts to feed the destitute. Meals were prepared and served to 8,100 people. A long line of waiting men stretched for blocks from the building all day. Shoes and clothing were also distributed. The men preparing the meals were lodgers themselves.

The refrigerated storage unit of the Municipal Lodging House is pictured around 1930. The large supplies of beef and lamb used to make the daily stew are visible. Also notice the large can of milk that was served at every meal.

Men at the lodging house prepare the stew for dinner around 1930. A certain number of lodgers helped in the preparation of each meal. In return for this work, they were given a noonday meal in addition to breakfast and dinner.

This is a section of the storage room at the Municipal Lodging House. Note the Jell-O, vegetables, horseradish, Worcestershire sauce, and other items of which the men's diets were comprised.

The dining room at the Municipal Lodging House proper is pictured in 1930. The supper menu consisted of the following foods: a meat course, which was beef or mutton stew, clam chowder, or franks and beans. In both the stew and the chowder there was a generous allotment of potatoes, carrots, turnips, onions, and tomatoes. Along with the meat course, lodgers were also served a portion of stewed fruit, apples, apricots, or peaches, bread, and coffee. This meal was always described by competent dieticians as well balanced. In the main kitchen of the Municipal Lodging House, most of the staff consisted of down-and-outers who were rewarded for their work by additional food and lodging and a token salary of $1 a day.

The spotless kitchen of the Municipal Lodging House was photographed around 1930. During this time in history, the lodging house had modern kitchen equipment, which was used to make wholesome food for thousands of jobless and hungry men and women.

The employees of the Municipal Lodging House celebrate St. Patrick's Day with dinner. The superintendent, Joseph A. Mannix, and his family lived at the lodging house because someone had to oversee the workings of the house 24 hours a day, seven days a week. The homeless and the jobless had to eat every day, allowing for no days off when shouldering the responsibility to feed New York's hungry people.

The dining room of the Municipal Lodging House on East 25th Street is pictured around 1940. The shelter was renovated under the term of Mayor Fiorello LaGuardia. The renovated building is clean, cheery, orderly, and warm. (New-York Historical Society.)

The dinner table is set for the superintendent's family and the assistant superintendent and his family around 1930. The men pictured are lodgers who worked at the Municipal Lodging House.

Harvey D. Gibson, head of the Emergency Unemployment Relief Committee, asked a lodger in bed at the Municipal Lodging House about the comfort of his bed and his meals around 1932. The lodger's reply was that he thought the bed was comfortable and he could not complain about the quality of his food. Pictured from left to right are a lodger, Supt. Joseph A. Mannix, Harvey Gibson, commissioner Frank Taylor, and Guy Emmerson.

The Municipal Lodging House was a six-story building. Four of those floors were gigantic dormitories, each consisting of approximately 100 beds.

This was the entrance to the second and third floors of the Municipal Lodging House, which were the two floors that housed the women's dormitories.

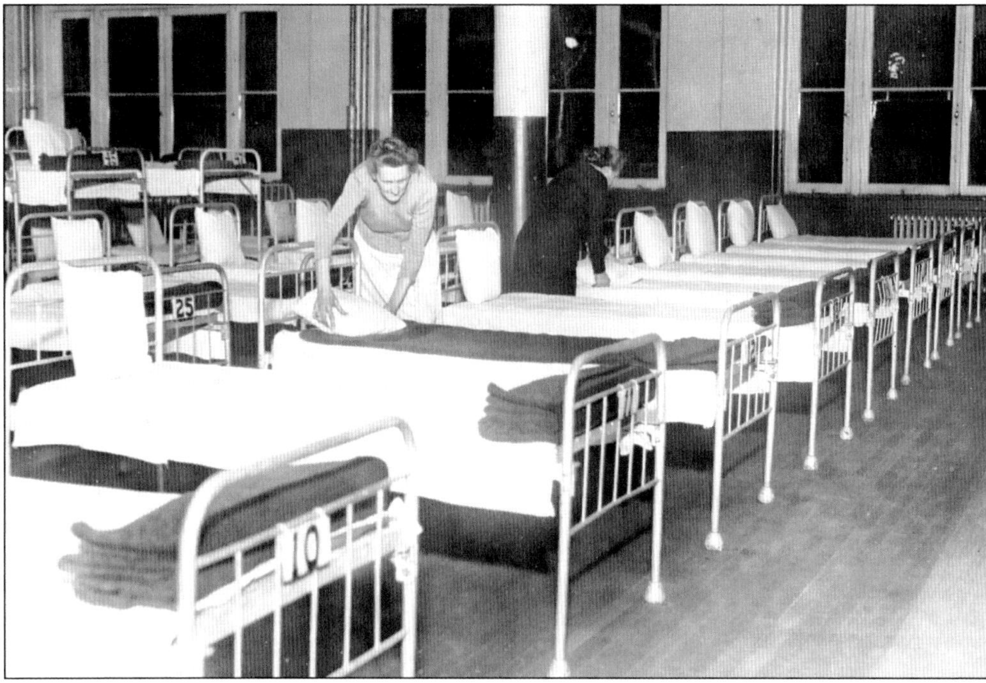

Mary Connelly is seen making the beds for the lodgers at the Municipal Lodging House around 1930. Connelly had an enormous task to accomplish every day, as she had 910 beds to make. Some of the lodgers also helped make up the beds daily.

Pictured is the women's dormitory in the Municipal Lodging House. Women lodgers had their own living quarters—the second and third floors of the lodging house proper. They also had their own dining room and a sitting room with a piano and a radio. The women were provided a sewing machine for their use and a laundry room where they could wash their own clothes.

Joseph A. Mannix (left) is seen shaking hands with Joe Cullen in 1931. Cullen was a friend to the homeless for 15 years. He died at the age of 58 in 1932. Assigned as a special officer to the Municipal Lodging House, Cullen was known as "Big Joe" to the homeless, as he was six feet tall and over 200 pounds. When he walked into a room, he was always given respectful attention. More than four million lodgers came under Cullen's guidance during his 15 years in the city service. It was said that if it were not for Cullen, many a hobo would have gone "bedless and foodless" after being turned away from the Municipal Lodging House for smoking in bed or some other infraction. Cullen gave his own money to the hobos for food and shelter, despite the fact that his yearly salary was $1,050. When Cullen died, Mannix arranged for his burial, as he died penniless and without relatives.

This c. 1930 photograph shows the 13th Precinct in Manhattan, where the Municipal Lodging House was located. Supt. Joseph A. Mannix is on the right wearing the derby. The policemen are standing outside Annex No. 1 and city pier No. 73 at the front of East 25th Street.

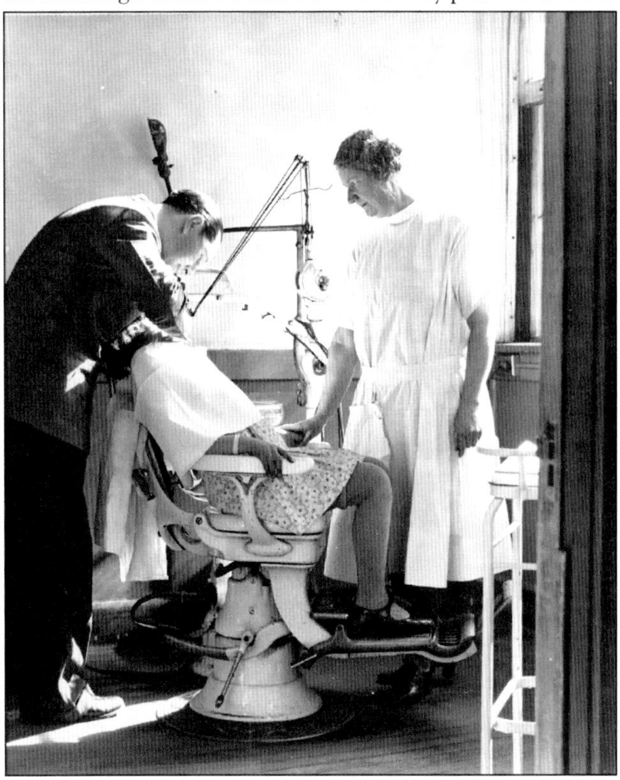

The Municipal Lodging House is shown around 1930. As seen in the picture, dental care was given to all the lodgers. It was one of the many services given to the homeless by the city.

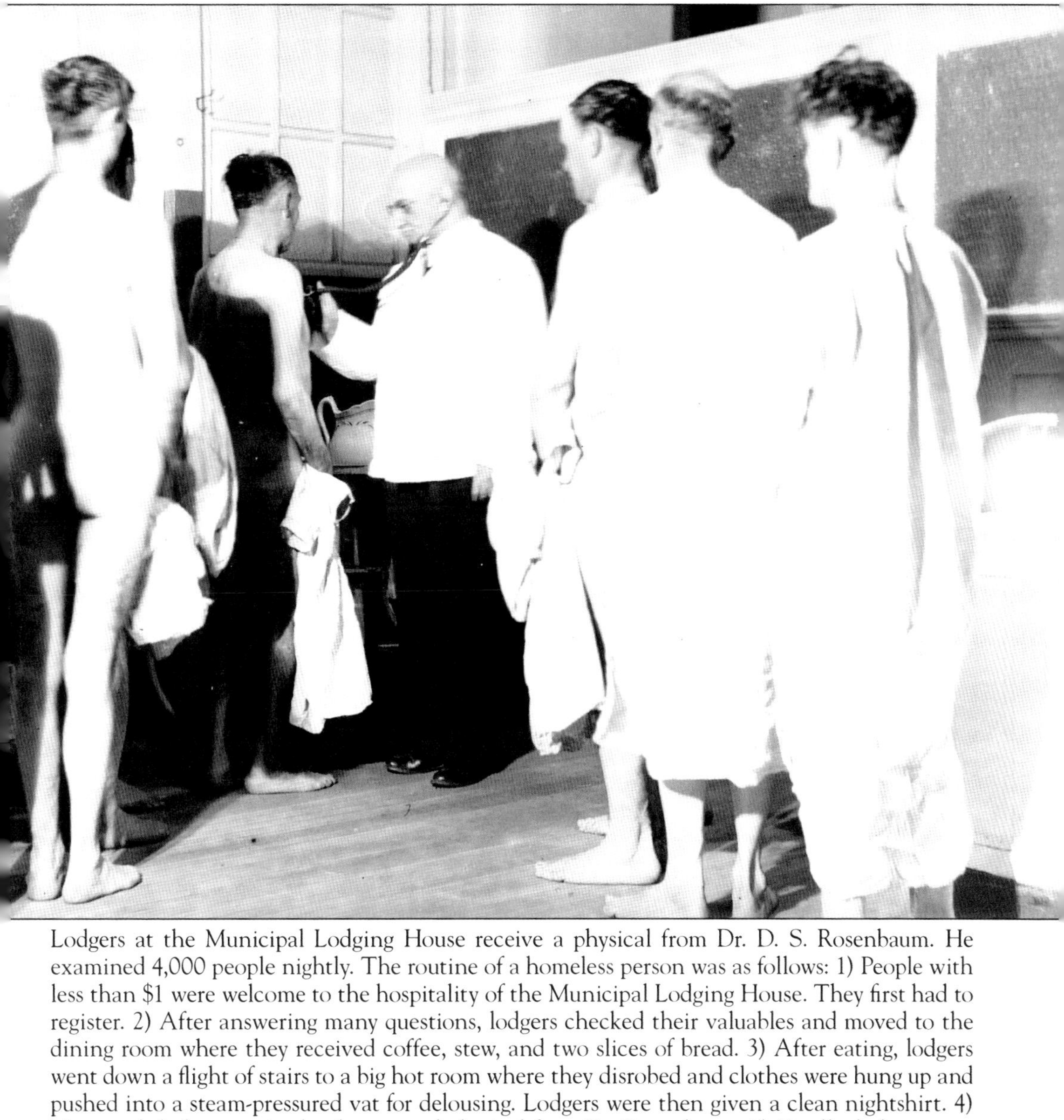

Lodgers at the Municipal Lodging House receive a physical from Dr. D. S. Rosenbaum. He examined 4,000 people nightly. The routine of a homeless person was as follows: 1) People with less than $1 were welcome to the hospitality of the Municipal Lodging House. They first had to register. 2) After answering many questions, lodgers checked their valuables and moved to the dining room where they received coffee, stew, and two slices of bread. 3) After eating, lodgers went down a flight of stairs to a big hot room where they disrobed and clothes were hung up and pushed into a steam-pressured vat for delousing. Lodgers were then given a clean nightshirt. 4) Next each lodger received a shower and physical from Dr. Rosenbaum. 5) Finally, lodgers were given a clean blanket and sent to the bedroom. 6) After a good night's sleep, lodgers awoke to a nutritious breakfast.

In January 1932, Aaron Weinstein and his family of 10 are sheltered at the Municipal Lodging House while Joseph A. Mannix, the superintendent, tries to find a job for him. Weinstein, a cap maker and resident of Brooklyn for 18 years, had taken his family to California for two years. For a time, several Weinsteins made small amounts of money in the movies, but unemployment finally led to their eviction from their Los Angeles home. Authorities bought them day coach tickets to New York and gave them $15. After staying at the Municipal Lodging House, their fellow New Yorkers found them an apartment and provided them with food, clothes, furniture, and the first two months' rent.

Pictured in 1935 are, from left to right, Joseph A. Mannix, superintendent of the Municipal Lodging House; boxer James Braddock, "Cinderella Man"; Joe Humphries, announcer at Madison Square Garden; boxer Sam Langford, "Boston Tar Baby"; and Arthur DeKuh. Mannix loved boxing and became friends with many boxers. In 1929, the Wall Street stock market crashed, and the ensuing depression hit New York City and the entire country. By 1934, one in four Americans was unemployed. Braddock lost all his assets in the crash. He was now a poor ex-prizefighter. When he could not pay his bills and take care of his family, he was forced to go on public relief and frequented the Municipal Lodging House for food and shelter. Braddock came back to win the heavyweight championship of the world. His story is chronicled in the movie *Cinderella Man*. The superintendent and the boxers are attending a smoker (fund-raiser for the local Catholic school and church). It was held at the Carmelite School Hall.

This photograph was taken in the Municipal Lodging House around 1940. Pictured are, from left to right, Joseph A. Mannix, David Rockefeller, and friend Rodman Gilder Jr. Standing behind Mannix are his two assistants. After completing a graduate course at the University of Chicago, David Rockefeller, son of John Rockefeller, took a tour of the Municipal Lodging House. Rockefeller was engaged in preparation for his doctor's thesis. He had been studying firsthand the workings of various city departments. Supt. Joseph A. Mannix and assistant superintendent John Gilligan gave Rockefeller a guided tour of the six-story terra-cotta building and its annex on pier No. 73. They ended their visit with a regular institutional meal.

This *c.* 1930 photograph shows road repairs on East 25th Street near the Municipal Lodging House. Notice the place where the lodgers wait to enter the lodging house on the right in the background.

Pictured in 1931 is the noonday meal line of the Municipal Lodging House on East 25th Street. The line stretched all the way down the street and was 5 to 10 men deep. Notice also that there are no women or children in line. Women and children were brought right into the house.

The large warehouse on the city pier at East 25th Street was opened as an annex to the Municipal Lodging House in 1930. The pier was located on the East River and was once used by the department of sanitation as a wharf for the loading of garbage scows and then by the police department as a garage for stolen vehicles. In 1930, the pier was dedicated by the commissioner of public welfare, Frank Taylor, to serve as an annex. The pier had 3,000 beds for the homeless and the facilities to feed 15,000 people daily.

Annex No. 1 of the Municipal Lodging House on pier No. 73 at East 25th Street is shown around 1930. Joseph A. Mannix, superintendent of the Municipal Lodging House, is in the center between his two assistants.

Annex No. 1, located at pier No. 73, housed men only and took the overflow from the Municipal Lodging House proper. There were 1,500 double-decked beds that accommodated 3,000 men nightly.

This long line of homeless men waits for dinner and shelter for the night outside Annex No. 1 on city pier No. 73 at the front of East 25th Street.

Pier No. 73 was located here in 1930 and was used as the annex to the Municipal Lodging House. The pier has long been torn down and replaced by a large office building, as seen in this October 2008 photograph. There seems to be no evidence left behind of the magnificent work done at this site by the welfare department of New York City during the Great Depression.

The breadlines of New York City are a widely recognized symbol of the Great Depression. The homeless and hungry lined up daily to enter the Municipal Lodging House proper and its annex at pier No. 73 on East 25th Street in Manhattan.

This c. 1932 photograph shows the bedroom of the Municipal Lodging House's Annex No. 1 on East 25th Street. This bedroom accommodated 3,000 men nightly. While it may not look like much, it provided warmth and refuge from the winter weather for many homeless New Yorkers.

Here is another view of the bedroom at Annex No. 1 at pier No. 73. Two lodgers converse before going to sleep. Notice the brass check around the neck of the man on the bottom bunk and the brass check on the wrist of the man on the top bunk. Every lodger was given two brass checks with identical numbers. He would put one check on his clothes that were being fumigated, and he wore the other check.

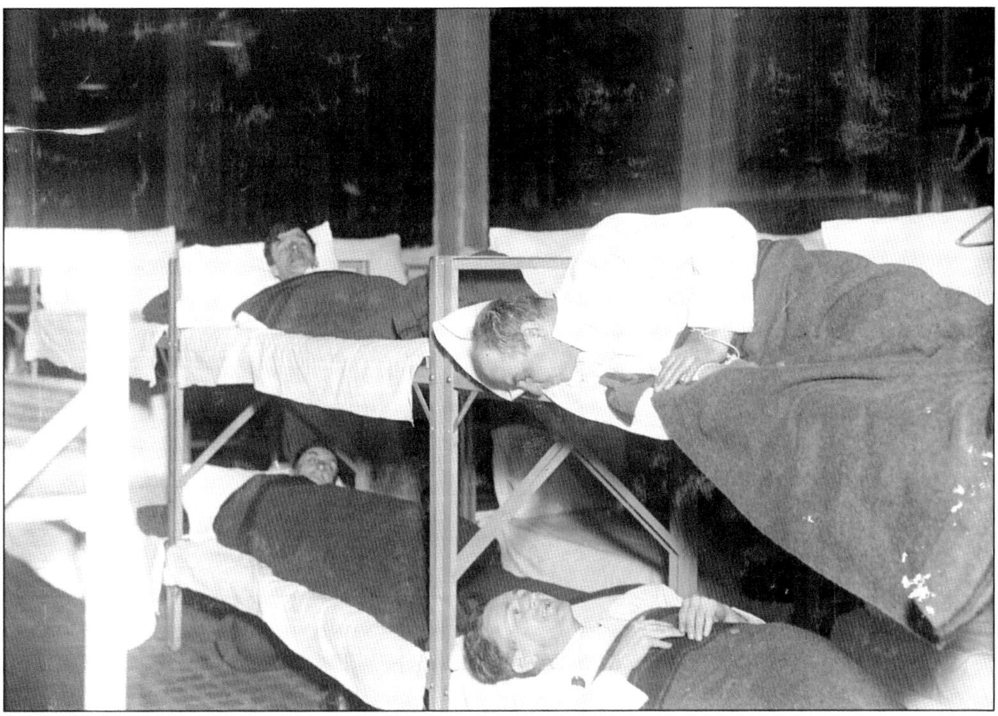

Pictured in November 1930 is the bedroom at the East 25th Street annex to the Municipal Lodging House. This picture appeared in the "Ripley's Believe It or Not!" column in the newspaper as the "largest bedroom in the world." There were 1,500 double-decked beds that accommodated 3,000 men nightly. The City of New York attacked the problem of caring for the needy in a big way by opening the East 25th Street annex.

Lodgers at Annex No. 1 are seen being served their evening meal.

The dining room of Annex No. 1 of the Municipal Lodging House is shown around 1931 while the homeless are eating their noonday meal. The men are served on the right and sit at picniclike tables in the center of the room.

This is the kitchen at the East 25th Street pier in 1930. The opening of the pier enabled the welfare department to serve 8,000 midday meals. The city could now feed 1,600 people an hour. Supt. Joseph A. Mannix outlined the means that the city would use to cope with what he called "a growing problem," stating, "Our policy will be to feed any hungry man first and to ask questions afterward."

This 1931 view of Annex No. 1 shows the kitchen where food is being served and the men eating in the dining room on the lower left.

At this time of giving, New York City shared its Christmas joy with the poor, the homeless, and the jobless. Some 10,000 men and women received their 1931 Christmas dinner at the Municipal Lodging House. The police glee club provided the entertainment.

Supt. Joseph A. Mannix reported that on January 1, 1931, 2,817 persons spent the night here at Annex No. 1. The breadline served 11,583 meals, the largest number since the kitchens were enlarged to serve 20,000 a day.

The Municipal Lodging House's Annex No. 2 was in the Manhattan terminal building of the old 39th Street Brooklyn ferry at the front of Whitehall Street, South Ferry, and is shown in January 1931. The bed capacity of the Municipal Lodging House proper for men, women, and children was 910. That of Annex No. 1 was 3,000 and that of Annex No. 2 was 1,946. Both annexes housed men only. Thus, the total of free beds furnished each night by the City of New York for the homeless, the unemployed, and other unfortunates was 5,856 beds. In 1932, according to Joseph A. Mannix's journal, about 4,300 homeless men showed up for free lodgings, as well as morning and evening meals, each day of the year. Men were supposed to apply for their night's lodging at the Central Registration Bureau at South Ferry. When applying to the Municipal Lodging House for food or shelter directly without going first to the Central Registration Bureau, they were given a night's lodging and food, but they were directed to go to the Central Registration Bureau for the homeless the next day.

This building is presently used as the Governors Island ferry house. In 1930, it was used as a ferry house, as Annex No. 2 to the Municipal Lodging House, and as the Central Registration Bureau office. This building has beautiful architecture. It was restored from 2002 to 2006.

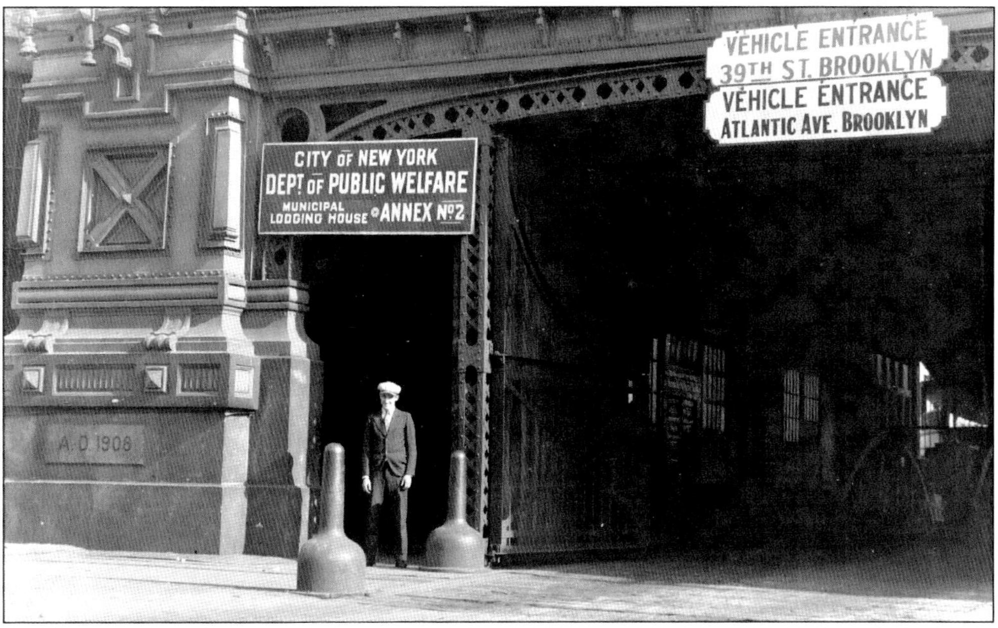

Above is the entrance to Annex No. 2 of the Municipal Lodging House in 1930. This annex was located at the Manhattan terminal building of the old 39th Street Brooklyn ferry at the front of Whitehall Street, South Ferry. This was the Central Registration Bureau where the homeless applied for lodging. Notice the cornerstone of the building that indicates it was built in 1908. It was a beautiful, ornate building that served many purposes.

This is the cornerstone of the Manhattan terminal building of the old 39th Street Brooklyn ferry at the front of Whitehall Street, South Ferry. The year 2008 marked the 100th anniversary of this building, which has been remarkably maintained over the years.

Pictured in October 2008 is the side of the Manhattan ferry terminal building at the front of Whitehall Street, South Ferry. This building is presently the Governors Island ferry house. In 1930, it was Annex No. 2 of the Municipal Lodging House. Besides serving as a ferry house, it was used for the overflow of the homeless from the Municipal Lodging House.

The admission office of Annex No. 2 of the Municipal Lodging House at South Street is pictured on March 10, 1931. The Central Registration Bureau was at South Ferry. Here the homeless were registered and given an identification card to be used when applying for admission to the shelter to which they were assigned. The men were also given two brass checks to be used for identification. Overseeing the applicants is Supt. Joseph A. Mannix (right). Registering this enormous amount of people successfully for food and shelter was an immense job carried out by the welfare department of New York City.

THE CLERK'S STORY

By JAY PARKER *

My "oomp" jest laffed when I took my seat,
And I smole a smile, 'twas such a great relief—
For the wooden stool I perched upon,
Had calloused my "aft" to a solid corn.
I've had many presents in my storm-tossed life—
From a Hobo-Bum or an erstwhile wife—
But among them all none can hold a place
To the Liver-pad cushion donated by Grace.

Its six o'clock and the work begins:
"What is your name?" "Oh-dam the din"
You say it is Pat? your surname too,
Born in Ireland? Hell yes—YOU.
How old are you Pat, just forty-five—
How long have you been here Oh man alive
Answer these questions: what is your job?
"Am a seaman Sir—Ex Navy Gob."
A Citizen? "Sure, 'bout twenty year—
Took out first papers when I reached the pier.
Was a Cop for awhile, but I got flat feet
And when the war came on, I joined the fleet."

* (at First-Time
windo

You're a Catholic—yes? And your eyes are brown,
(But the hair has slipped from the top o' your crown)
Of medium height— build is spare—
Do you eat onions? (Ah! what do I care.)
Now who did you work for, Pat, last time,
What was the name of the Steam Ship line?
O. K., and the boat was the S. S. "Rover"
And they signed you off when you docked at Dover?
Where do you live Pat w'en your'e on land—
At 25 South Street when you got the sand!

Well one question more and I'll pass you in—
What is the name of your nearest kin?
Your father name was Patrick too?
His address and that will do.
You say he is dead, well wher'd he go—
Straight up to Heaven or down below?
So I give 'im his checks and say "go eat"
And turn to the next and the show repeat.
We interview men from every clime
And close up shop at late bed time.

This *c.* 1930 poem was written by Jay Parker and describes a welfare worker's daily job of registering lodgers into the Municipal Lodging House. He tells of all the questions that were asked of each homeless person in order to stay at the shelter. The clerk's questions include "name, age, place of birth, married, religion, last job, citizenship, and for how long, and next of kin."

At the Central Registration Bureau at South Ferry in 1931, the homeless were registered and given an identification card to be used when applying for admission to their assigned shelter. If a homeless person was assigned to the Municipal Lodging House at East 25th Street, he was given food and shelter there on that night. On subsequent nights he was assigned to either of the other annexes.

Applicants who sought shelter at the Central Registration Bureau stood in line at the window on which the beginning letter of their last name was posted.

Employees of the welfare department of New York City register the homeless for shelter at the Municipal Lodging House and its annexes in 1931. Each lodger was asked his name, age, birthplace, number of years in the United States and New York City, last address he called home, last place he was employed, his normal occupation, war service (if any), whether married or single, and the name of a relative or friend to be notified in case of an emergency.

Applicants stand in line to register for shelter at the Central Registration Bureau at South Ferry in 1931.

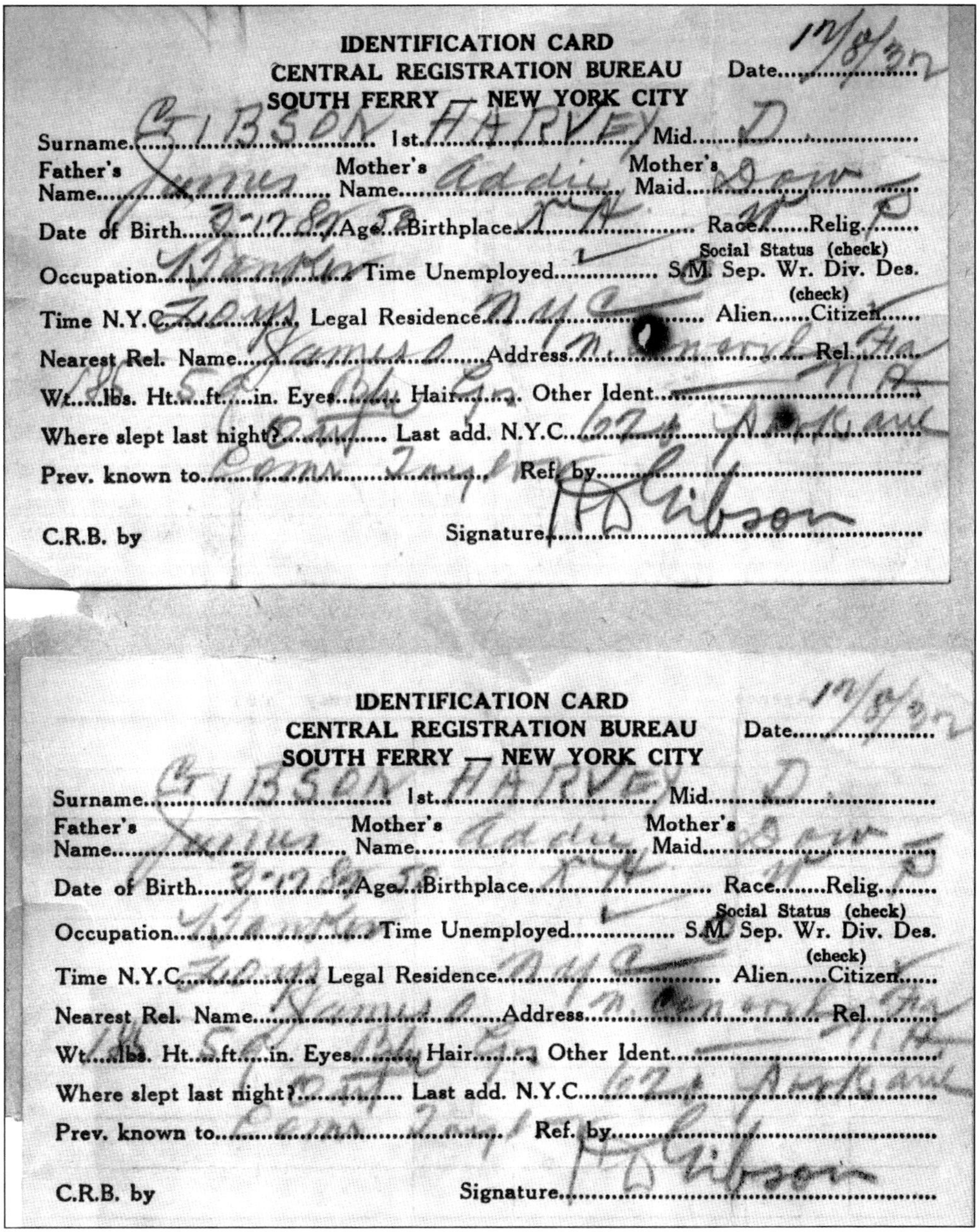

IDENTIFICATION CARD
CENTRAL REGISTRATION BUREAU
SOUTH FERRY — NEW YORK CITY

Date 12/8/32

Surname Gibson 1st Harvey Mid D
Father's Name James Mother's Name Addie Mother's Maid
Date of Birth Age Birthplace Race Relig
Occupation Banker Time Unemployed Social Status (check) S. M. Sep. Wr. Div. Des.
Time N.Y.C. Legal Residence (check) Alien Citizen
Nearest Rel. Name Address Rel.
Wt. lbs. Ht. ft. in. Eyes Hair Other Ident.
Where slept last night? Last add. N.Y.C.
Prev. known to Ref. by
C.R.B. by Signature H D Gibson

IDENTIFICATION CARD
CENTRAL REGISTRATION BUREAU
SOUTH FERRY — NEW YORK CITY

Date 12/8/32

Surname Gibson 1st Harvey Mid D
Father's Name James Mother's Name Addie Mother's Maid
Date of Birth Age Birthplace Race Relig
Occupation Banker Time Unemployed Social Status (check) S. M. Sep. Wr. Div. Des.
Time N.Y.C. Legal Residence (check) Alien Citizen
Nearest Rel. Name Address Rel.
Wt. lbs. Ht. ft. in. Eyes Hair Other Ident.
Where slept last night? Last add. N.Y.C.
Prev. known to Ref. by
C.R.B. by Signature H D Gibson

Harvey D. Gibson, chairman of the Emergency Unemployment Relief Committee, registered as a first-time lodger at the Municipal Lodging House. These are the actual registration cards filled out by Gibson. He was doing a surprise inspection of the shelters with the permission of Frank Taylor, commissioner of public welfare, to determine how well the shelters were being run. He found the shelters to be in excellent condition and agreed that the private relief committee would take care of any overflow of homeless for the municipal shelters. Gibson and Taylor worked together so that it would be impossible for any homeless resident of New York to go without food or shelter.

City officials return valuables to the lodgers as they are checking out in this 1930 photograph. Annex No. 2 was at the Manhattan terminal building of the old 39th Street Brooklyn ferry at the front of Whitehall Street, South Ferry. Each lodger has a brass check in his hand to claim his belongings. He was given this brass check when he registered.

The dormitory at South Ferry is shown around 1930.

Pictured around 1930 is the first floor of Annex No. 2 of the Municipal Lodging House.

New York City's Battery Park ferry terminal on the East River is pictured around 1930. The large New York City ferries went to St. George on Staten Island, while the smaller Coast Guard ferries went to Governors Island. These terminals have long been renovated.

The municipal ferry terminal was built in 1908 during the term of Mayor George McClellan. A politician, statesmen, and educator, McClellan served as mayor of New York City from 1904 to 1909. During his term of office as mayor, the first subway opened. This plaque, pictured in 2008, is found inside one of the ferry gates.

Doctors and nurses give physicals to lodgers at Annex No. 2 of the Municipal Lodging House around 1931. The staff also helped fill out registration forms. The annex was located on the upper floor of the municipal ferry terminal, at the foot of Whitehall and South Streets on the East River. This terminal was constructed during the McClellan administration.

This political cartoon illustrates the homeless waiting in line at the Municipal Lodging House's Annex No. 2. The unknown artist calls it "Roosevelt's Draft Army—1939" because one of the main reasons the county pulled out of the Great Depression was the enlistment of all the unemployed in America at the beginning of World War II. This, along with Franklin D. Roosevelt's work programs (Civil Conservation Corps, WPA), helped bring an end to the Great Depression.

The kitchen in Annex No. 2, like Annex No. 1 and the Municipal Lodging House proper, was always kept spotless. The kitchens were run by the lodgers who wanted to earn their way instead of taking a handout.

Food is being served to the homeless at Annex No. 2. The men are so hungry that only one man notices the photographer. The welfare department of New York managed to feed the large numbers of hungry and homeless by opening two annexes to the Municipal Lodging House. (New-York Historical Society.)

New York City's Battery Park ferry terminal is pictured around 1930. This ferry terminal was on the East River, and it has long since been renovated. As can be seen, the New York skyline has significantly changed since 1930.

Supt. Joseph A. Mannix (left) and his friend Jerry Vogel provide entertainment at the Municipal Lodging House at Christmas 1930. During holidays, Vogel spent countless hours entertaining the poor. He had many connections in the entertainment field and enlisted such talents as Jimmy Durante, Rudy Vallée, noted jazz composer W. C. Handy, well-known radio singer Dick Robinson, and Frank LaMonta's Orchestra.

In May 1931 at Annex No. 1, Jerry Vogel and his friends entertain the lodgers. Jerry and his gang spent their free time at insane asylums, public hospitals, and the Municipal Lodging House, bringing candy, cigarettes, records, and other items to spread cheer. Having grown up poor, Vogel remembered a kind family making his Thanksgiving happy. He swore he would do the same for other unfortunate people.

Above is an autographed music sheet given to Supt. Joseph A. Mannix by W. C. Handy. Handy was a noted African American jazz composer and father of St. Louis blues and Memphis blues. Handy and Rudy Vallée, along with several other performers, entertained 6,500 homeless people on Christmas 1930 at the Municipal Lodging House.

Joseph A. Mannix (left) and Jerry Vogel stand in front of the pier on East 25th Street around 1930. Pictured in the background are the lodgers coming for shelter and an evening meal.

Theodore Metz, a well-known musician and entertainer, is pictured distributing Old Gold cigarettes to the homeless in 1931. He spent many hours of his free time helping the less fortunate. Notice the lodgers in the background going for their noonday meal at the Municipal Lodging House annex on East 25th Street.

Jerry Vogel, publisher and distributor of sheet music, is seen with his musical entertainer friends in 1931. They are on East 25th Street to entertain the homeless at the Municipal Lodging House.

Theodore Metz is pictured in 1931. He wrote "Hot Time in the Old Town Tonight." He played this song and "Bread Line Blues" for the men of the Municipal Lodging House. Assisted by Jerry Vogel, Metz furnished the entertainment for the noonday meal of the unemployed. Metz came to the United States in 1879 to get a job as a pharmacist, but he got sidetracked playing a violin in a saloon for $3 a night. Later he toured the country as a bandleader for McIntyre and Heath Minstrels. For a short time, Metz made the homeless faces smile at the Municipal Lodging House. Also photographed in 1931 are three ladies from Jerry Vogel's gang that performed for the homeless in the lodging house.

Pictured on May 10, 1931, are two performers from Jerry Vogel's gang who volunteered their time to make the lives of the homeless men of the Municipal Lodging House a little more enjoyable. In the background are the breadlines on East 25th Street. Also pictured are two members of Jerry Vogel's gang standing in front of the Municipal Lodging House prior to entertaining the homeless men. These people gave up their free time to make the lives of the less fortunate more bearable.

Two performers from Jerry Vogel's gang perform for the homeless men at the Municipal Lodging House on May 10, 1931. Also pictured are three members of Jerry Vogel's gang standing in front of Annex No. 1. Notice the line of unemployed individuals in the background.

Joe Daniels (left), an entertainer and newspaperman, was part of Jerry Vogel's gang, which entertained the lodgers on May 10, 1931. He was one of the greats of the Lindy Hop at the Savoy Ballroom in Harlem. Roy Smeck (below) is also pictured in May 1931. In the background can be seen the men waiting in line to eat. Smeck was part of Jerry Vogel's gang. A talented musician, he was born in February 1900 in Pennsylvania. His skill on the banjo, guitar, steel guitar, and ukulele earned him the nickname "Wizard of the Strings." Smeck was invited to play at the inaugural celebration for Franklin D. Roosevelt in 1932 and at the London Palladium for the coronation of King George VI in 1937.

Another musician associated with Jerry Vogel's gang performs at the Municipal Lodging House in 1931. The men in the picture are the Manhattan Towers Hotel Orchestra.

CITY OF NEW YORK
THE MAYOR'S OFFICIAL COMMITTEE

JAMES J. WALKER, CHAIRMAN
MAYOR
CHARLES A. BUCKLEY, TREASURER
CITY CHAMBERLAIN
THOMAS F. McANDREWS, SECRETARY
SECRETARY TO MAYOR

346 BROADWAY
SEVENTH FLOOR

TEL.: BARCLAY 8700

For release SATURDAY Dec 20, 1930

Luck takes strange turns.

One of the strangest twists of all will occur to-morrow ~~xxxx~~- sun- when William C. Handy, noted Negro jazz composer, father of "Memphis Blues", "St. Louis Blues" and other "blues" and 'jes as blue as he can be comes down to the Municipal Lodging House of the New York City Department of Public Welfare, foot of East 25th street.

Handy, will join Rudy Vallee, Dick Robinson, well-known radio singer, Frank La Monta's orchestra, Jerry J. Vogel and others in staging Christmas time entertainment for probably 6500 jobless and homeless persons - the City's guests.

Handy will then be playing free for a ~~xxxxxxxxxxx~~ "millionaire pauper" in the crowd who in other days once paid Handy $ 4,000 for an evening's entertainment at Carnegie Hall.

This man is Robert Clairmont, poet, writer, owner of nearly $ 1,000,000 before the stock market crash and now a resident in the Municipal Lodging House, it was revealed yesterday -fri- by Joseph A. Mannix, superintendent of the lodging house.

Just fifteen months ago, Clairmont was worth $ 800,000 in stocks, he told Mannix. The market collapsed and the poet sold out barely in time to salvage the last $ 3,000 of his margin.

- more -

This news release was sent to the newspapers on December 20, 1930, from Mayor Jimmy Walker's office. The release describes a man named Robert Clairmont who was a millionaire before the stock market crash of 1929. Clairmont was a poet and a writer before he lost his fortune. He had spent $10,000 on his last Christmas party, and now he was celebrating Christmas at the Municipal Lodging House. W. C. Handy, a noted composer, heard of Clairmont's poor luck and decided to entertain at the Municipal Lodging House. Clairmont had once paid Handy $4,000 for one evening's entertainment at Carnegie Hall.

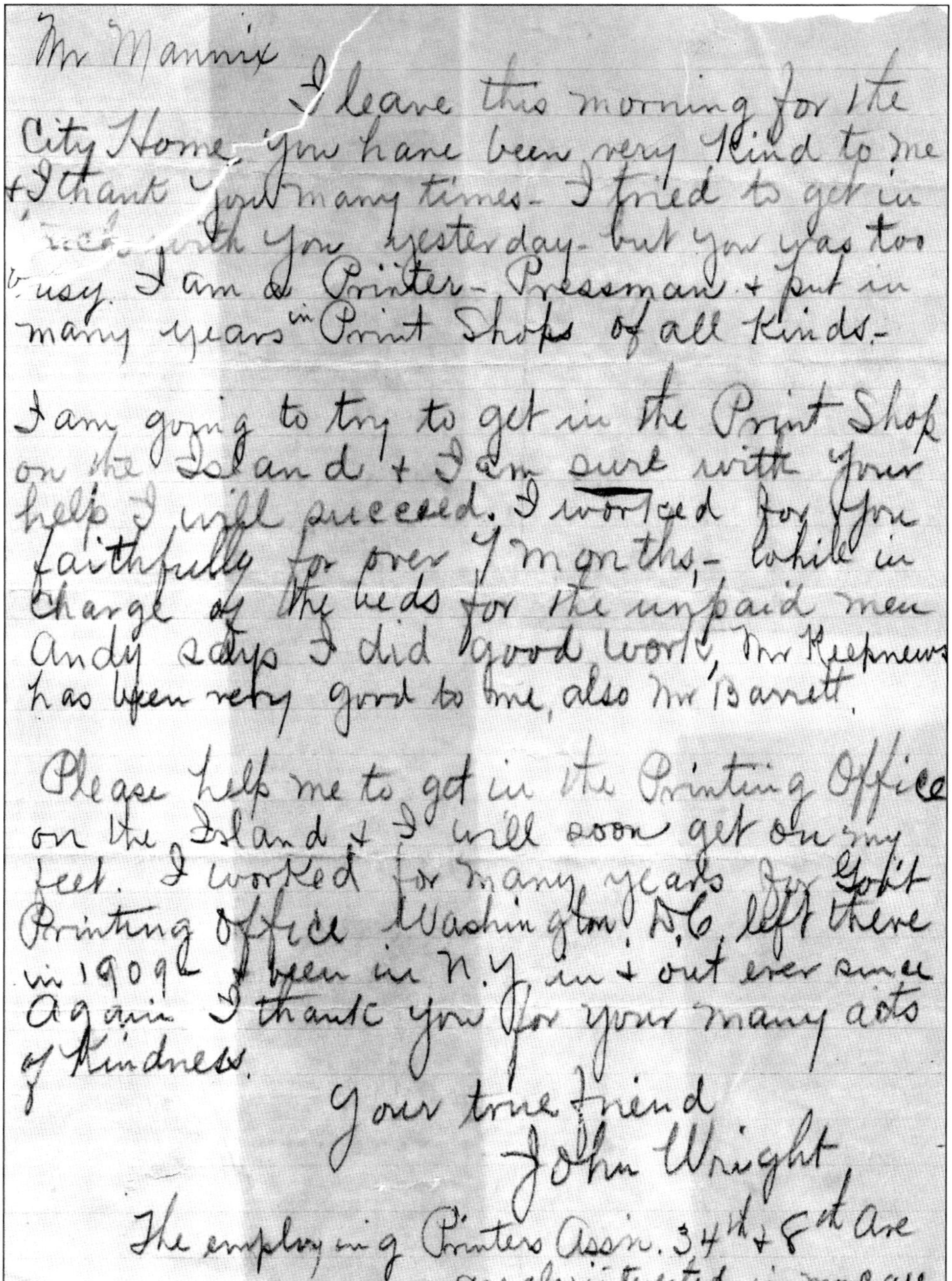

Mr Mannix

I leave this morning for the City Home, you have been very kind to me + I thank you many times. I tried to get in [illegible] with you yesterday but you was too busy. I am a Printer - Pressman + put in many years in Print Shops of all kinds.-

I am going to try to get in the Print Shop on the Island + I am sure with your help I will succeed. I worked for you faithfully for over 7 months,- while in charge of the beds for the unpaid men Andy says I did good work, Mr Keepnews has been very good to me, also Mr Barrett.

Please help me to get in the Printing Office on the Island + I will soon get on my feet. I worked for many years for Gov't Printing Office Washington D.C. left there in 1909 + been in N.Y. in + out ever since. Again I thank you for your many acts of kindness.

Your true friend
John Wright

The employing Printers Assn. 34th + 8th Ave are also interested in my case.

This letter to Supt. Joseph A. Mannix was written by former lodger John Wright on August 8, 1931. The letter thanks Mannix for his kindness while Wright was at the lodging house and asks for help getting into the printing office on City Island. Wright was more or less asking for a recommendation to attain his new position. This letter is a fine example of the mind set of most people during the Great Depression. People wanted to work for their food and shelter, but there just were not any jobs. When given employment, many lodgers tried to pay the city for its kindness. Proof of this are the many thank-you letters sent to the superintendent.

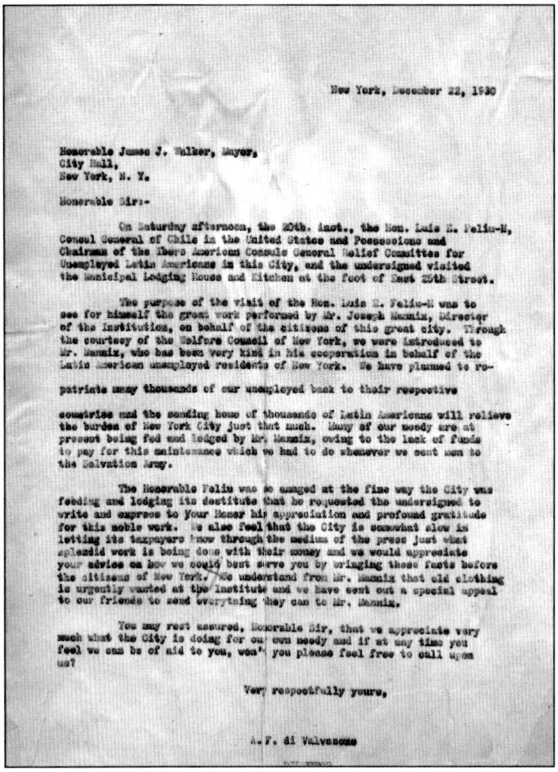

New York, December 22, 1930

Honorable James J. Walker, Mayor,
City Hall,
New York, N. Y.

Honorable Sir:-

On Saturday afternoon, the 20th. inst., the Hon. Luis E. Feliu-M, Consul General of Chile in the United States and Possessions and Chairman of the Ibero American Consuls General Relief Committee for Unemployed Latin Americans in this City, and the undersigned visited the Municipal Lodging House and Kitchen at the foot of East 25th Street.

The purpose of the visit of the Hon. Luis E. Feliu-M was to see for himself the great work performed by Mr. Joseph Mannix, Director of the Institution, on behalf of the citizens of this great city. Through the courtesy of the Welfare Council of New York, we were introduced to Mr. Mannix, who has been very kind in his cooperation in behalf of the Latin American unemployed residents of New York. We have planned to repatriate many thousands of our unemployed back to their respective countries and the sending home of thousands of Latin Americans will relieve the burden of New York City just that much. Many of our needy are at present being fed and lodged by Mr. Mannix, owing to the lack of funds to pay for this maintenance which we had to do whenever we sent men to the Salvation Army.

The Honorable Feliu was so amazed at the fine way the City was feeding and lodging its destitute that he requested the undersigned to write and express to Your Honor his appreciation and profound gratitude for this noble work. We also feel that the City is somewhat slow in letting its taxpayers know through the medium of the press just what splendid work is being done with their money and we would appreciate your advice on how we could best serve you by bringing these facts before the citizens of New York. We understand from Mr. Mannix that old clothing is urgently wanted at the Institute and we have sent out a special appeal to our friends to send everything they can to Mr. Mannix.

You may rest assured, Honorable Sir, that we appreciate very much what the City is doing for our own needy and if at any time you feel we can be of aid to you, won't you please feel free to call upon us?

Very respectfully yours,

A. F. di Valvasone

A. F. Valvasone wrote this letter to Mayor Jimmy Walker to compliment the city's welfare department and particularly the Municipal Lodging House for the excellent manner in which they took care of the homeless. Hon. Luis Feliu, consul general of Chile, visited the Municipal Lodging House and kitchen at the foot of East 25th Street. Feliu was very impressed by the manner in which the Latin American unemployed residents were treated in New York, and he insisted that Valvasone write to the mayor and express his appreciation and profound gratitude for his noble work. Many foreign dignitaries, as well as lodgers themselves, sent letters of appreciation to New York City's welfare department.

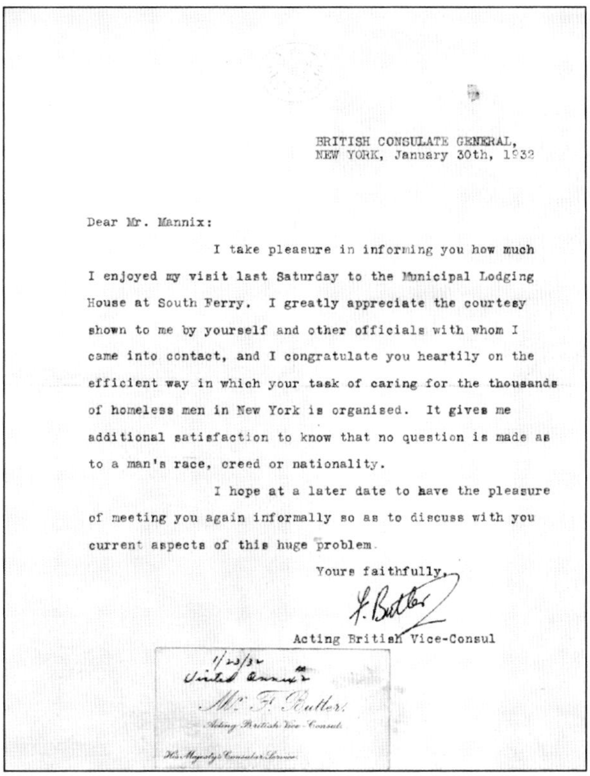

BRITISH CONSULATE GENERAL,
NEW YORK, January 30th, 1932

Dear Mr. Mannix:

I take pleasure in informing you how much I enjoyed my visit last Saturday to the Municipal Lodging House at South Ferry. I greatly appreciate the courtesy shown to me by yourself and other officials with whom I came into contact, and I congratulate you heartily on the efficient way in which your task of caring for the thousands of homeless men in New York is organised. It gives me additional satisfaction to know that no question is made as to a man's race, creed or nationality.

I hope at a later date to have the pleasure of meeting you again informally so as to discuss with you current aspects of this huge problem.

Yours faithfully,

F. Butler

Acting British Vice-Consul

Mr. F. Butler
Acting British Vice-Consul
His Majesty's Consular Service

This is a letter written to Supt. Joseph A. Mannix from the British vice consulate general on January 30, 1932. The letter thanks Mannix for his hospitality during a recent visit to the Municipal Lodging House. It also congratulates him on the fine and efficient manner in which he performs his task of caring for thousands of New Yorkers with no regard for race, creed, or nationality.

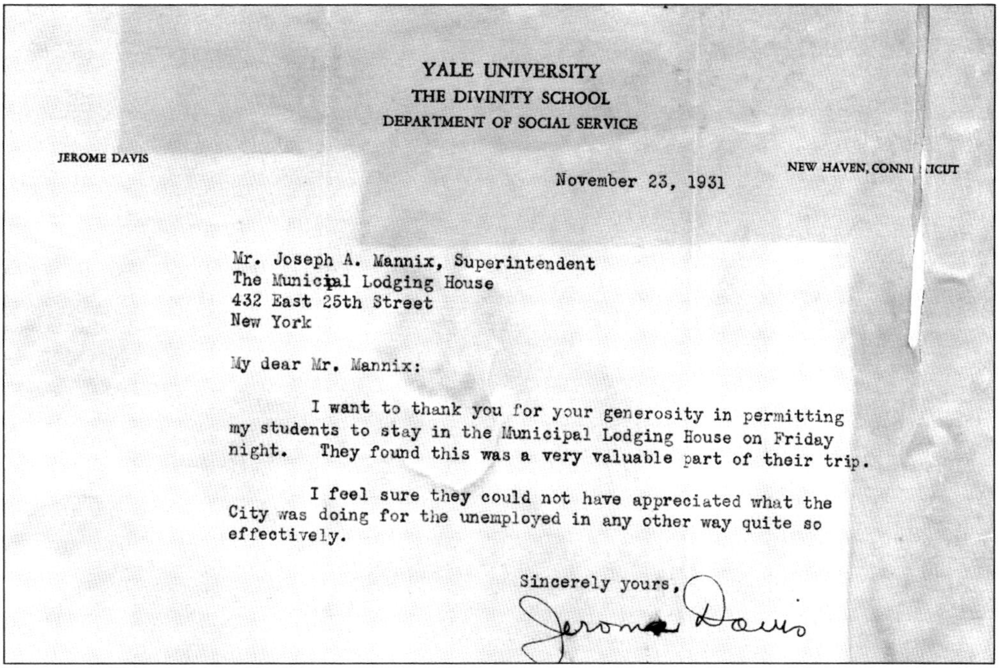

YALE UNIVERSITY
THE DIVINITY SCHOOL
DEPARTMENT OF SOCIAL SERVICE

JEROME DAVIS

NEW HAVEN, CONNECTICUT

November 23, 1931

Mr. Joseph A. Mannix, Superintendent
The Municipal Lodging House
432 East 25th Street
New York

My dear Mr. Mannix:

I want to thank you for your generosity in permitting my students to stay in the Municipal Lodging House on Friday night. They found this was a very valuable part of their trip.

I feel sure they could not have appreciated what the City was doing for the unemployed in any other way quite so effectively.

Sincerely yours,
Jerome Davis

Above is a letter written to Supt. Joseph A. Mannix from Yale Divinity School director Jerome Davis. Davis wrote to thank Mannix for allowing his students to see firsthand how the welfare department of New York helped the homeless in an organized and humane manner.

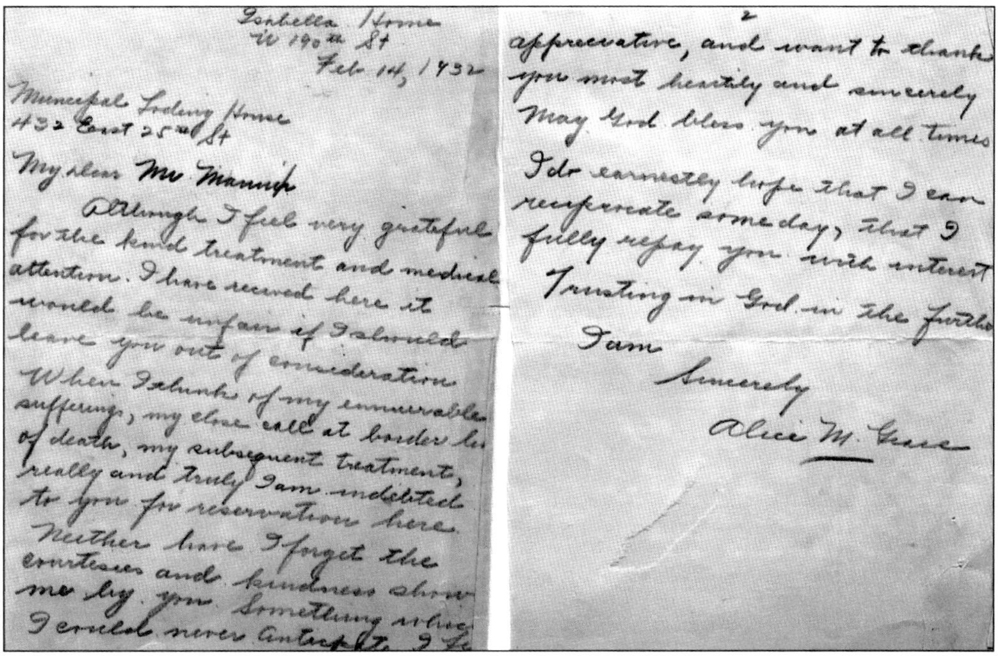

Isabella Home
W 190th St
Feb 14, 1932

Municipal Lodging House
432 East 25th St

My dear Mr Mannix

Although I feel very grateful for the kind treatment and medical attention. I have received here it would be unfair if I should leave you out of consideration. When I think of my innumerable sufferings, my close call at border line of death, my subsequent treatment, really and truly I am indebted to you for reservation here. Neither have I forget the courtesies and kindness shown me by you. Something which I could never [illegible] I fe

2

appreciative, and want to thank you most heartily and sincerely May God bless you at all times I do earnestly hope that I can reciprocate some day, that I fully repay you with interest Trusting in God in the further

I am
Sincerely
Alice M. Grace

Alice Grace wrote to Supt. Joseph A. Mannix in 1932 thanking him for sending her to the Isabella Home for treatment. She was very appreciative of the manner in which Mannix recognized her difficulties and sent her to a place that would care for her. It was part of his job to make sure that every person was treated individually and given the best of care.

NEW YORK URBAN LEAGUE, INC.

FOR SOCIAL SERVICE AMONG NEGROES

202-6 WEST 136TH STREET, NEW YORK CITY

TELEPHONES: EDGECOMBE 4-9600-1-2

"NOT ALMS BUT OPPORTUNITY"

JAMES H. HUBERT
EXECUTIVE DIRECTOR

July 12, 1932

Mr. Joseph E. Mannix, Superintendent
Municipal Lodging House
East Twenty-fifth Street
New York City

My dear Mr. Mannix:

Many thanks for your letter with regard to the visit of Mr. Lancaster and his offer of co-operation. Both as Director of the League and a member of the Co-ordinating Committee on Unemployment, I have had occasion to know of the splendid work you are doing to aid homeless and unemployed men. It has been a pleasure for us to co-operate with you, and I can say, without hesitation, that never has there come any complaint whatever from our men regarding the treatment received at the Municipal Lodging House, based on color. Apparently, your entire Staff treat all men according to their merits. This, in my opinion, is something that we all should appreciate, especially when there come to us so many reports of discrimination due to race.

Believe me.

Very truly yours,

James H. Hubert

Executive Director.

JHH:S

James Hubert, executive director of the New York Urban League, wrote to Supt. Joseph A. Mannix thanking and commending him for the kindly manner in which he and his staff treated all men at the shelter regardless of race. Credit should be given to the staff and the welfare department for the humane way they treated the homeless and unemployed.

COPY
BEN HOWE
280 East 21st
Brooklyn, N.Y

September 28th, 1932

Commissioner Frank J. Taylor,
50 Lafayette Street,
New York City.

My dear Commissioner:

At your suggestion I called on Mr. Joseph A. Mannix Superintendent of the Municipal Lodging House at 438 East 25th St, and our Committee was shown over the premises by him.

I feel I would be remiss in my civic duty if I do not compliment the Department of Welfare on the conditions prevailing at this shelter for our unfortunates. I can assure you that we can all sleep sounder in our beds when we hear this winter's winds knowing that these men and women are cared for so compassionately.

I have one slight criticism to make which is entirely constructive, and perhaps not within your power to grant in these days when Budget has the gripes. I am a little afraid that the men's menu dues not give them sufficient vitamins and mineral ash. The adequate protein and carbohydrate diet that they get is all that could be desired, but they do need fruit or raw cabbage slaw, or tomatoes.

I say this in the interest of economy, because a man living continuously on this diet is certainly on the way to the Hospital. I am quite sure that any expert dietician will agree with me. It is not economical to care for men in the hospital. A little raw cabbage added to the diet that I saw the men get, is the most economical step the City could take.

After thirty years of experience in social work of one kind and another, I expected to have the usual sinking of heart when I met Mr. Mannix. Men in charge of such Institutions it seems almost invariably get a penitentiary guard face on them in spite of all they can do. Mr. Mannix is a decided exception to this almost universal rule. There is a sweetness and kindness about this man's nature and bearing that I think the citizens of New York should be made cognizant of. It would add a qualitative something to the citizenship of each of them to know that our unemployed fellow citizens are under the care of a man who is inately the gentleman.

Mr. Mannix is working with us to solve the problem of the unmarried veteran. If you will be patient a few days we hope to have some plan that will meet with your approval. Thank you for your courtesy and forebearance in these discussions.

I am,

Sincerely,

(Sgd) Ben Howe
Temporary Chairman
Veterans Housing Committee

Ben Howe, temporary chairman of the Veterans Housing Committee, wrote this letter on September 28, 1932, to commissioner Frank Taylor, commending him, his welfare department, and Supt. Joseph A. Mannix on the fine and efficient manner in which they cared for the homeless. The Municipal Lodging House was the last refuge for the unemployed and homeless. Howe continues by complimenting Mannix for being a fine gentleman who does his job and shows compassion for his fellow man.

Copy

September 13, 1932.

Hon. Frank J. Taylor,
Commissioner of Public Welfare,
50 Lafayette Street,
Manhattan, New York City.

My dear Commissioner:-

Last night I went through the municipal lodging house on East 25th Street.

I feel that I should say a word of commendation for the splendid work the City is doing in taking care of unfortunate men and women who have no place to sleep or eat. The lodging house seems to be very well managed and operated, and it undoubtedly tends to a mitigation of crime.

May I be permitted to congratulate you upon your efficient operation of the lodging house, and may I say a word for your superintendent, Mr. Joseph A. Mannix, who seems to be untiring in his effort to give the best serviees in him.

I feel that his faithful and efficient services should be commended.

Very truly yours,

Thomas Flosevoor

County Judge, Richmond County.

TFC/ED.

Above is a letter written by county judge Thomas Flosevoor to commissioner Frank Taylor of the welfare department commending the department and Supt. Joseph A. Mannix on their splendid work taking care of the unemployed in the city.

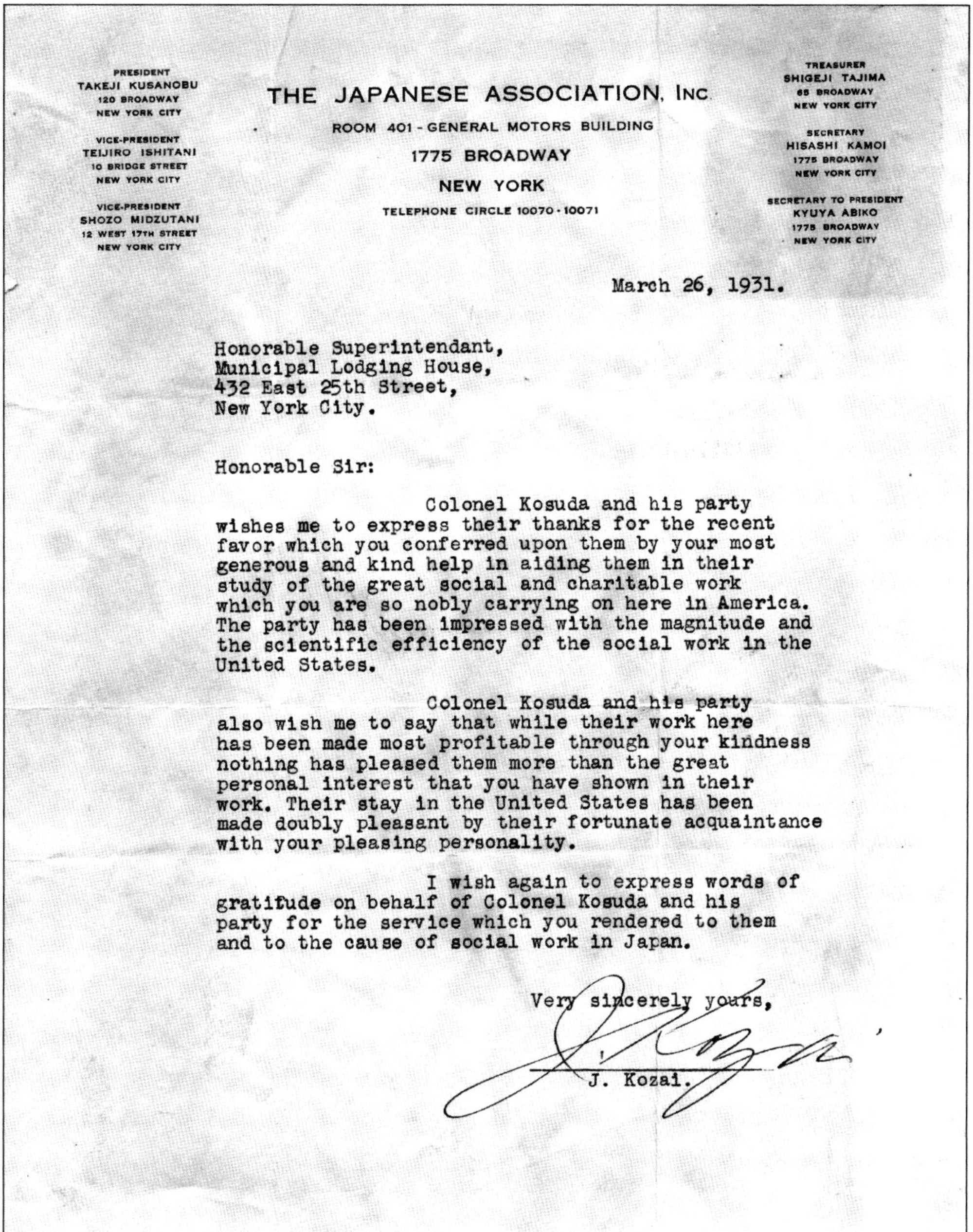
PRESIDENT
TAKEJI KUSANOBU
120 BROADWAY
NEW YORK CITY

VICE-PRESIDENT
TEIJIRO ISHITANI
10 BRIDGE STREET
NEW YORK CITY

VICE-PRESIDENT
SHOZO MIDZUTANI
12 WEST 17TH STREET
NEW YORK CITY

THE JAPANESE ASSOCIATION, INC.
ROOM 401 - GENERAL MOTORS BUILDING
1775 BROADWAY
NEW YORK
TELEPHONE CIRCLE 10070 - 10071

TREASURER
SHIGEJI TAJIMA
65 BROADWAY
NEW YORK CITY

SECRETARY
HISASHI KAMOI
1775 BROADWAY
NEW YORK CITY

SECRETARY TO PRESIDENT
KYUYA ABIKO
1775 BROADWAY
NEW YORK CITY

March 26, 1931.

Honorable Superintendant,
Municipal Lodging House,
432 East 25th Street,
New York City.

Honorable Sir:

Colonel Kosuda and his party wishes me to express their thanks for the recent favor which you conferred upon them by your most generous and kind help in aiding them in their study of the great social and charitable work which you are so nobly carrying on here in America. The party has been impressed with the magnitude and the scientific efficiency of the social work in the United States.

Colonel Kosuda and his party also wish me to say that while their work here has been made most profitable through your kindness nothing has pleased them more than the great personal interest that you have shown in their work. Their stay in the United States has been made doubly pleasant by their fortunate acquaintance with your pleasing personality.

I wish again to express words of gratitude on behalf of Colonel Kosuda and his party for the service which you rendered to them and to the cause of social work in Japan.

Very sincerely yours,

J. Kozai.

Jiro Kozai of the Japanese Association thanked Supt. Joseph A. Mannix for the kindness the Japanese delegation was shown during a visit to New York to study the great social and charitable work being done there. The Japanese government used New York's welfare programs as a model for its programs in Japan.

In a ceremony at the central office on September 1, 1955, commissioner Crystal Potter congratulates Supt. Joseph A. Mannix on his 40th anniversary in city service. Mannix, a native of Greenwich Village, was the son of a fireman. He joined the department of public charities in 1915. He came up through the ranks in the New York City Department of Welfare, where he was appointed supervisor of the Municipal Lodging House in 1928. Since that time, he administered various programs of the Bureau of Institutional Administration, including Camp LaGuardia for homeless men in Orange County and the rehabilitation center for homeless men on Hart Island (from 1950 to 1954). His career was only interrupted by his enlistment during World War I. From a young man, Mannix dedicated his life to helping the unfortunate people of New York City. In his office at the shelter on East 3rd Street, there hung a plaque that read one word: *others*. Ever since he was a child, Mannix wanted to help others. This was the creed he followed all through his life.

Two

Tammany Hall and Tenement Housing during the Depression

Tammany Hall was the Democratic political machine that dominated New York City from Fernando Woods's mayoral victory in 1854 to the election of Mayor Fiorello LaGuardia in 1934. Tammany's power and influence lasted 80 years. It was not until the drastic social and cultural changes brought on by the Great Depression that Tammany fell from power.

In 1932, Mayor Jimmy Walker was forced to step down from office for being under investigation for corruption in his administration. Walker, a politician of Tammany Hall, was accused of vice racketeering (an illegal scheme to profit from prostitution). During Tammany's reign of power, the immigrant population in New York was dependent on it for jobs. At the same time Walker resigned, Franklin D. Roosevelt's New Deal restricted immigration and made people less dependent on Tammany jobs.

After Walker resigned, both parties chose a more progressive candidate, Fiorello LaGuardia. When LaGuardia took office, he cleaned house, eliminating jobs given to people in exchange for favors or votes. He replaced the old corrupt Tammany system with a new civil service led by men of merit. During his term of office, LaGuardia fought a public war against racketeers and gamblers and was committed to rebuilding the city's housing and public health facilities. LaGuardia's relationship with Roosevelt helped New York City become the New Deal's showcase for all America.

Those fortunate enough to have employment and the ability to pay rent instead of being homeless and frequenting the Municipal Lodging House likely lived in a tenement building. A tenement was a multiple-family dwelling, and most of the city's immigrant families resided in them. Tenement homes had three classes. The cheapest apartment was in the attic and was a one-room apartment usually rented by an elderly person. The second class was a three-room apartment owned by the very poor. The three rooms consisted of a kitchen and two bedrooms. The third class had four rooms that were rented by working-class people. During the Great Depression, poverty and the decrease of the construction of new housing led to the major overcrowding of the city's tenement buildings.

The Tammany Hall building on 14th Street in Manhattan is pictured around 1930. Located in the arch at the top of the building is a marble statue of Tamanend, a chief of one of the clans that made up the Lenni-Lenape Nation in the Delaware Valley at the time when Philadelphia was established. Tamanend developed peaceful relations between the Native Americans and the English settlers. After his death in 1698, Tamanend became a national folk hero and a national symbol for the new country. Tammany societies sprang up all over the country. The most famous of these was New York City's Society of St. Tammany, which grew into the large Democratic machine known as Tammany Hall. Tammany Hall's electoral base was the large immigrant population in New York City. In exchange for their votes, Tammany granted favors to the immigrants. Tammany Hall became the charitable institution immigrants turned to when they needed help with citizenship, jobs, or money for food and rent. In 1929, Tammany Hall moved from 14th Street to Union Square and 17th Street. (New-York Historical Society.)

The Academy of Music on 14th Street and Irving Place, shown around 1920, was a theater and an opera house. Built in 1854, it seated about 1,500 people. The academy burned in a fire and was rebuilt in 1866. Recognized as the first successful opera house in the United States, the academy also housed political rallies, charity balls, and science and industry fairs. This building was demolished in 1926 and a Con Edison building was built on the site. (New-York Historical Society.)

Manhattan's 14th Street is pictured in the early 1900s. Tony Pastor's theater was in the same building as Tammany Hall. Pastor, a singer and songwriter from Brooklyn, produced variety shows to draw middle-class families to the theater. In his final years, he fought against national theater chains for the rights of local showmen, earning him the nickname of "Little Man Tony." (New-York Historical Society.)

Above is an early-1900s picture of Tammany Hall. Next door to Tammany Hall is a burlesque hall featuring Benny Leonard, the greatest lightweight fighter in the world. Nicknamed "Ghetto Wizard," Leonard retired in 1924 and lost his entire fortune in the stock market crash of 1929. In 1931, he resumed fighting and made public appearances to earn money. (New-York Historical Society.)

A politician in Tammany Hall, Mayor Jimmy Walker visits Welfare Island on November 13, 1938. Walker's visit was broadcast over the radio on WMCA. Welfare Island, formerly known as Blackwell's Island and later known as Roosevelt Island, is a narrow island in the East River. Throughout the 19th century, various hospitals, asylums, and correctional institutions were located on the island. The Welfare Island penitentiary was closed in 1935 upon the completion and opening of the Rikers Island prison. Walker, pictured in the center, is surrounded by other politicians and staff of the facilities on Welfare Island.

Mayor Jimmy Walker, on the right, is pictured around 1930 helping the lodgers by serving the noontime meal. Walker was a flamboyant and somewhat corrupt mayor of New York City. Walker's term of office was known for the proliferation of speakeasies. There were many investigations of corruption during his administration, which eventually led to his resignation.

Democratic delegates to the national convention in New York City for Al Smith are seen in 1924. Smith was attempting to win his party's nomination for president of the United States. The front-runners at the convention were Smith and William Gibbs McAdoo. The Ku Klux Klan, which was very popular at the convention, opposed Smith because he was a Roman Catholic. Neither of the front-runners won, as John W. Davis secured the party's nomination.

In 1924, Democrats are seen heading to the Democratic convention at Madison Square Garden. The third man from the left is Joseph A. Mannix, superintendent of the Municipal Lodging House. This convention was also nicknamed the "Klan bake" because of the influence of the Ku Klux Klan. John W. Davis won his party's nomination, but he lost the election to Pres. Calvin Coolidge.

Hon. John G. Bennett (left), attorney general of New York, and Hon. Alfred E. Smith head to Franklin D. Roosevelt's inauguration in 1933. Smith was born in 1873 in New York City and was elected governor four times. He was instrumental in the completion of construction of the Empire State Building during the Great Depression. Bennett served as New York State attorney general from 1931 to 1942.

On March 4, 1933, the Anawanda Club delegation of New York, a Democratic club in the city, heads to the inauguration of Roosevelt. The delegation is seen waiting for the train in Pennsylvania Station.

The Anawanda Club delegation is on its way to Franklin D. Roosevelt's inauguration in Washington, D.C., in 1933. The superintendent of the Municipal Lodging House, Joseph A. Mannix, was one of the delegates to the inauguration.

The Tammany Hall delegation awaits the opening of gates at Pennsylvania Station to board two 17-car trains to Washington, D.C., to attend the March 3, 1933, inauguration of Franklin D. Roosevelt. Roosevelt campaigned against Herbert Hoover in the 1932 presidential election. Roosevelt's first address took on a very solemn quality, as by 1933 America was deep in the Great Depression.

Two Democrats from Tammany Hall are pictured at the inauguration of Franklin D. Roosevelt in Washington, D.C. The man on the left is H. Warren Hubbard, commissioner of the department of public works, and on the right is Patrick Halloran, deputy sheriff of New York County.

Louis McNally (left), superintendent of City Home on Welfare Island, and Joseph A. Mannix, superintendent of the Municipal Lodging House, are pictured at the Roosevelt inauguration. These men were part of the Tammany Hall delegation to the inauguration of the president in Washington, D.C.

The Tammany Hall delegation to the inauguration of Franklin D. Roosevelt is shown in 1933. Pictured here are, from right to left, Mayor John O'Brien of New York City, David Rendit, John F. Curry, Judge Darlington, and an unidentified delegate. After Mayor Jimmy Walker was forced to resign from office due to corruption charges, O'Brien finished his term of office. O'Brien is credited with restoring order to the city's finances. He served one year in office and was not reelected to a second term. A three-time delegate to the Democratic National Convention, he died in September 1951.

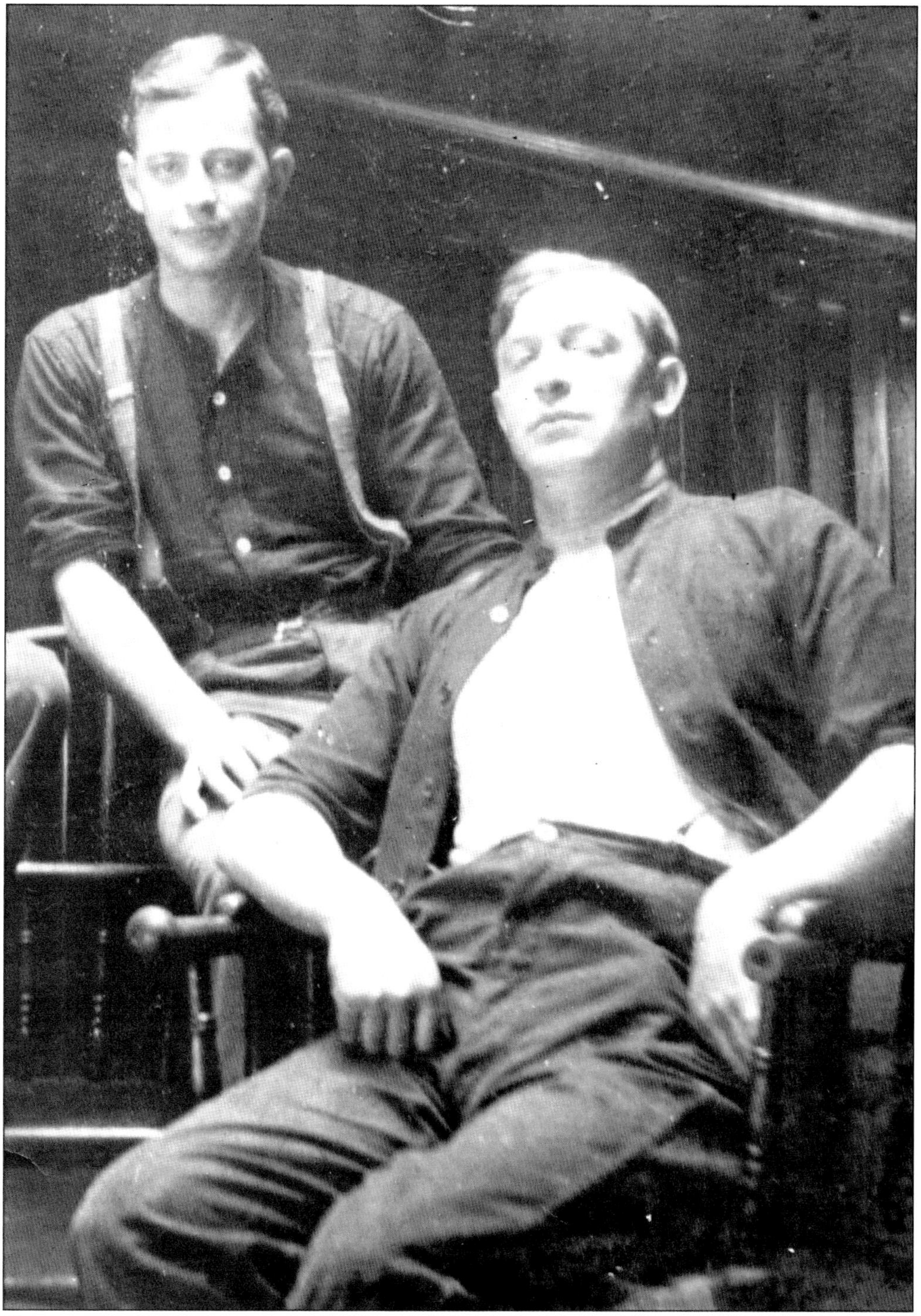

Shown around 1920 is Martin Gabriel Mannix, father of Joseph A. Mannix. Martin was a New York City fireman and also district captain of the Jefferson Democratic Club. Martin, on the right, is seen with another fireman in their firehouse. Joseph A. Mannix, like his father, made his life's work helping the citizens of New York City.

A "ghetto newsboy" was photographed on the Lower East Side around 1930 by Irving Browning. During the Depression, the elderly were forced to work to survive. The term *ghetto* originally meant an area in the city in which Jews were confined. (New-York Historical Society.)

Irving Browning captured this scene on Sixth Avenue in 1930. The men pictured are reading through job postings outside an employment agency. Men would check the postings daily in hopes of finding a job. (New-York Historical Society.)

Irving Browning captured this woman selling pickles on a New York City street around 1930. As pickles cost between 1¢ and 5¢ each and street vendors pushed these heavy wooden carts around 12–14 hours a day, this was difficult work to make only a few cents a day. (New-York Historical Society.)

This *c.* 1930 Lower East Side street scene was captured by Irving Browning. Pictured are the tenement houses and vendor pushcarts selling everything from food and clothing to household items. This view was a typical scene in New York City during the Depression. (New-York Historical Society.)

This man sells apples on the street for 5¢ around 1930. People in New York City were forced to sell and peddle food or clothing to survive the Depression. (New-York Historical Society.)

Men of all ages were unemployed during the Depression, and they searched daily for employment. Pictured in this *c.* 1930 Irving Browning photograph are idle men sitting in the streets reading newspapers and looking for employment. (New-York Historical Society.)

A shantytown on Twelfth Avenue and 40th Street was photographed around 1930 by Irving Browning. Shanties were makeshift houses made by the unemployed in the city. Shantytowns were nicknamed Hoovervilles after the president who was blamed for the Depression. (New-York Historical Society.)

Pictured in this *c.* 1930 Irving Browning photograph are three men in a shanty on Riverside Drive. People were forced to live in these make-shift homes during the Depression. These three men numbered their shanty, as can be seen in the picture. At one time in their lives they had jobs and homes and now they had neither. (New-York Historical Society.)

Another shantytown on Twelfth Avenue and 40th Street was photographed around 1930 by Irving Browning. The man in the shanty is offering his friend something to eat from a frying pan. His home is made from an old billboard advertising a movie starring William Powell on the right and Joe E. Brown on the left. (New-York Historical Society.)

Mary Gallagher and her daughter Mildred are pictured in 1930. The Gallagher family immigrated to New York from Ireland. Notice the tenement building on the right in the background. During this time period, Tammany Hall was the Democratic political machine. Tammany's electoral base consisted mainly of the immigrant population. In exchange for their votes, Tammany gave the immigrants a means of physical existence: food, rent money, and employment. Tammany is linked with the rise of the Irish in American politics. Beginning in the 1800s, Tammany's bosses grew rich by illegal means. The most famous of all was Boss Tweed, who won the New York State Senate election but was eventually sent to jail for stealing. It is estimated that Tweed and his associates stole anywhere from $400 million to $2 billion.

Eva Jones, an Irish immigrant, poses in front of Central Park in April 1936. Central Park was built in the middle of the 19th century when Tammany Hall was in power under Boss Tweed. The sheep in the park had to be removed and sent upstate for fear that the homeless and starving people would eat them. Some 20,000 workers were needed to build the park, and it took 15 years to complete.

Pictured during the 1930s are May Jones and her three children: Evelyn, age three, Mildred, age one, and Willie, age six months. They were one of the city's many Irish immigrant families. Jobs were scarce in the 1930s, and women had to do their fair share of work to help support their families. Many Irish women took in laundry to earn some income.

Members of an Irish immigrant family are pictured in their tenement around 1930. The family came to New York looking for work but found overcrowding and unemployment.

Matthew and Mary Gallagher, Irish immigrants, are seen in 1930. Immigrants faced many hardships in New York City during the Depression. There was a scarcity of jobs, food, and money for rent. The immigrants took great pride in coming to America and were very excited about becoming citizens of the United States.

Above is an Irish immigrant family in New York City. In the picture are a man and wife and their little daughter. Notice the laundry in the background hanging from building to building. This was a regular sight at the tenement buildings during the Depression.

This Irish immigrant family settled in New York City in the early 1900s. The little boy is Frederick Matthew Gallagher, and he is surrounded by his father, uncles, and family friends during a picnic in the park in the 1930s.

Young boys play on a fire escape on the Lower East Side in this *c.* 1930 photograph by Arnold Eagle. Eagle was a Hungarian immigrant who came to New York City in 1929. In 1932, he joined the Film and Photo League, an organization devoted to documentary photography and newsreels. In 1935, he joined the WPA as a photographer, and he produced documentary studies of New York City slums and the Second Avenue el. He also freelanced for many magazines, including *Fortune* and the *Saturday Evening Post*. In 1948, he worked as a cinematographer on documentary films. In later life, he taught filmmaking at the New School for Social Research. His pictures depict the hard and dreary life of New Yorkers during the Depression and also show the character and strength of a people trying to survive the worst economical period of modern times in the country. Arnold Eagle died in Manhattan at the age of 82. (Lower East Side Tenement Museum, Arnold Eagle Collection.)

Arnold Eagle is pictured on top of a heap of metal scraps outside a Lower East Side tenement building in 1935. This photograph was taken when Eagle worked for the WPA, and like many of his other works, it shows loneliness and poverty, just like the times in which he lived. (Lower East Side Tenement Museum, Arnold Eagle Collection.)

A young boy eats an ice-cream cone while sitting on a trash can on the Lower East Side around the 1930s. Notice the boarded-up windows of the shop and the graffiti, which was a sign of the times. (Lower East Side Tenement Museum, Arnold Eagle Collection.)

Three children sit on a Lower East Side fire escape around 1935. The laundry hanging on the line was a typical sight during this time. The mother is not pictured and is not watching her children. Children at that time learned to become independent at an early age. (Lower East Side Tenement Museum, Arnold Eagle Collection.)

A shoemaker is pictured in his store on East 20th Street in 1939. Many immigrants arrived in New York City and applied their skills to a trade to survive. During the Depression, people had to work 12–14 hours a day to earn a living. During this time, people were independent and willing to work long hours so they could take care of themselves. They were a proud people and would rather work the whole day than be placed on public assistance. (Lower East Side Tenement Museum, Edward Schwartz Collection.)

Men sit among pushcarts on the Lower East Side during the 1930s. The pushcarts sold everything from food to household items. Notice the brooms and soaps. The man in the hat is buying fresh fruit. In the background are tenement buildings. (Lower East Side Tenement Museum, Arnold Eagle Collection.)

This Lower East Side street scene was captured around 1935 and shows many conditions of the Depression in the city. Visible are the tenement buildings, street vendors, women socializing at the pushcarts, and children playing on the sidewalks. The people used the fire escapes for more living space. (Lower East Side Tenement Museum, Arnold Eagle Collection.)

Three boys and a girl in a communion dress stand outside an Italian grocery store on the Lower East Side around the 1930s. The young girl appears to be posing for the picture, and the boys seem to be little rascals with smirks on their faces. (Lower East Side Tenement Museum, Arnold Eagle Collection.)

A young boy sits looking out over a *c.* 1930s tenement yard littered with trash on the Lower East Side. (Lower East Side Tenement Museum, Arnold Eagle Collection.)

This *c.* 1930s view from a tenement window shows hanging laundry, an empty lot, and the street below. This photograph seems to be Arnold Eagle's attempt to show the world from the eyes of those living in the midst of the Depression struggles. (Lower East Side Tenement Museum, Arnold Eagle Collection.)

Pictured in the 1930s are two Italian shopkeepers in their grocery store on the Lower East Side. During the Depression nothing was fancy. The grocery store contained just food, no frills. These grocers used every bit of space. Notice the cheese and meats hanging from the ceiling. (Lower East Side Tenement Museum, Arnold Eagle Collection.)

A woman is shown in her housedress around 1935. She lived in a tenement house, and it appears that she has just given someone, probably a child, a bath in the bathtub she is leaning on. During the Great Depression, people did not have separate rooms for their tubs. They bathed in the living room. (Lower East Side Tenement Museum, Arnold Eagle Collection.)

In 1935, a young girl sits alone on a stairway in a Lower East Side tenement. (Lower East Side Tenement Museum, Arnold Eagle Collection.)

A young girl sits alone on the Lower East Side in 1935. The despair and loneliness on the little girl's face reflect the conditions of the Depression. In his photographs, Arnold Eagle captured the economic, social, and political hardships of city residents. It is interesting to note that while the little girl looks sad she is not crying. This tough life likely made this generation independent and self-reliant. (Lower East Side Tenement Museum, Arnold Eagle Collection.)

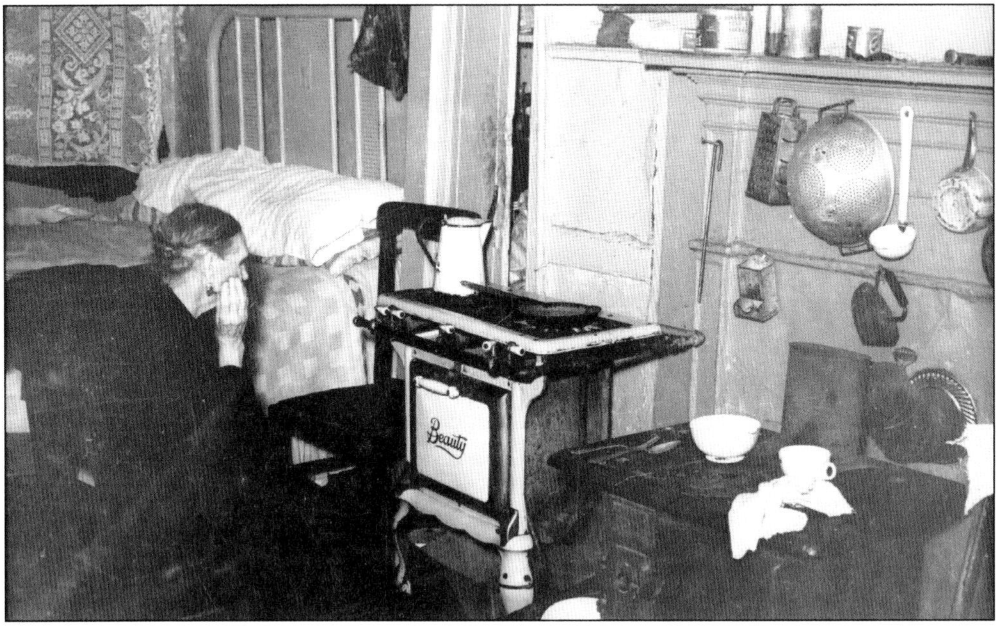

Arnold Eagle captured this elderly woman sitting in her one-room apartment on the Lower East Side in 1935 during his work with the WPA. The WPA was the largest New Deal agency developed by Franklin D. Roosevelt in 1935. It gave millions of Americans jobs and income during the Great Depression. The WPA was the largest employment base at that time. (Lower East Side Tenement Museum, Arnold Eagle Collection.)

A toddler stands in the kitchen of a Lower East Side tenement in 1935. Visible in the kitchen are the bare necessities of life: water, food, and a heat source—the potbellied stove in the center of the room. (Lower East Side Tenement Museum, Arnold Eagle Collection.)

Three

Camp LaGuardia and Hart Island

Camp LaGuardia opened as a shelter for the homeless in New York City in 1934. The purpose for the camp was to provide temporary shelter in a healthy environment as compared to the dreary life of the streets on New York City. Camp LaGuardia had the advantage of rehabilitation and restoration of morale and habits of work. Camps such as LaGuardia were an essential part of any temporary relief program. The residents of the camp were recruited from the Municipal Lodging House—homeless and forlorn who had stayed beyond their time at the institution. They were gathered up in buses and transported to Camp LaGuardia. Arriving at the camp, they found fresh air and the opportunity to work and farm, thus giving them a purpose in life. The camp closed in 2007 and became the property of Orange County. The reason for the closing of New York's largest shelter for the homeless was because the city wanted to move toward a more permanent solution to the homeless problem.

Hart Island, a small island in the Long Island Sound, has been used as a workhouse, a hospital, a Civil War internment camp, a rehabilitation camp for homeless men, a Nike missile base, and a potter's field for the City of New York. It was used as a rehabilitation home for 2,000 men in 1950 when Joseph A. Mannix was the director.

This c. 1934 photograph shows the main building at Camp Greycourt. Commissioner Ben Howe, of the welfare department of New York, believed that it was not enough to give the unfortunates bed and bread. The unemployed needed a purpose in life; they needed a job and a reason to get up in the morning, and Camp Greycourt gave this to the men.

Camp Greycourt, pictured around 1934, was a 326-acre farm colony owned by the City of New York in Orange County. The men in the picture had farmed the land and grown the potatoes and are now peeling them for dinner. Seven hundred homeless men from the Municipal Lodging House had been given a new purpose in life. They got up every morning and had a job to do.

This photograph was taken around 1934 at the Greycourt train station. Greycourt is situated 65 miles north of New York City on the uplands of Orange County. The welfare department of New York City decided to experiment and start a farm colony for the unemployed men of the Municipal Lodging House.

Pictured around 1934 are some residents of Camp Greycourt in Orange County. The camp was renamed Camp LaGuardia in 1935 after the exuberant New York City mayor Fiorello LaGuardia. During the first year of operation, 150 men worked on the farm. Pictured here are seven of the residents getting ready to farm the land. Notice the antiquated farm tools.

Some of the farm buildings of Camp Greycourt are pictured around 1934. Notice the residents working the farm. The beautiful scenery makes it clear why the men would prefer looking at the Catskills and the green open fields rather than the drab city streets of New York City.

In 1934, the first detachment of 200 men was sent to the former women's farm colony at Greycourt. Camp Greycourt, later named Camp LaGuardia, was going to be able to house 1,000 homeless and jobless men from the Municipal Lodging House. Pictured here are some of the residents planting potatoes.

Pictured around 1934 are some of the residents of Camp Greycourt constructing drainage ditches around the main building. In the background are Camp Greycourt's fields and the Catskill Mountains.

Camp LaGuardia is pictured as it is today. Camp LaGuardia opened as a shelter for the homeless in New York City in 1934 to provide temporary shelter in a healthy environment as compared to the dreary life of the streets in New York City. The camp closed in 2007 and became the property of Orange County.

Pictured in October 2008, Camp LaGuardia closed in 2007 to allow New York to move toward more permanent housing for the homeless. The camp's main building is pictured in the center of the photograph. Today no one is permitted on the grounds.

This 1934 photograph shows the buildings at Camp Greycourt used as dormitories for the jobless men from the Municipal Lodging House of New York City during the Great Depression. Before 1934, this camp was a prison for women.

Pictured in 1934 are New York City Department of Welfare employees evaluating the work to be completed at Camp Greycourt.

A lone Camp Greycourt resident returns from work to eat dinner in 1934. All the farm buildings used for the farm colony are seen in the background. To grow crops in Upstate New York, all the slate had to be removed from the soil. This task was performed by the homeless men from the Municipal Lodging House.

The residents of Camp Greycourt rake the lawn in front of the main building at the camp in 1934. In the background are the Catskill Mountains.

Welfare commissioner Ben Howe is seen speaking to the residents of Camp Greycourt (later Camp LaGuardia) from the camp's main building in 1934. Howe felt it was important to provide the men a chance to earn a living and feel useful.

This c. 1934 photograph shows the main building at Camp Greycourt. Opened in 1934, the camp was situated at the site of a woman's prison. In 1935, it was named after Mayor Fiorello LaGuardia. The old jail cells in the main brick building housed only older, frailer men, although most men were assigned a cot and a squat locker in dormitory-style rooms in other buildings.

This photograph was taken at Camp Greycourt in Orange County in 1934. The residents of the camp are bringing their bed linens to the laundry before going to work. The camp tried to teach the men to be self-sufficient. The Catskill Mountains in the background made for a lovely setting for the men to live and work in.

In the spring of 1934, 200 men from the Municipal Lodging House were picked up by bus and transported to a farm colony called Camp Greycourt. This camp was later renamed Camp LaGuardia. By the end of 1934, 1,000 men were residents of the camp. The men worked on the farm and were paid $1 a day. The men in the photograph are clearing the field.

Pictured in 1934 are the grounds of Camp Greycourt. The 300-plus acres at the camp made it New York City's largest homeless shelter. It was the only one surrounded by farms and trees. In the background are the majestic Catskill Mountains.

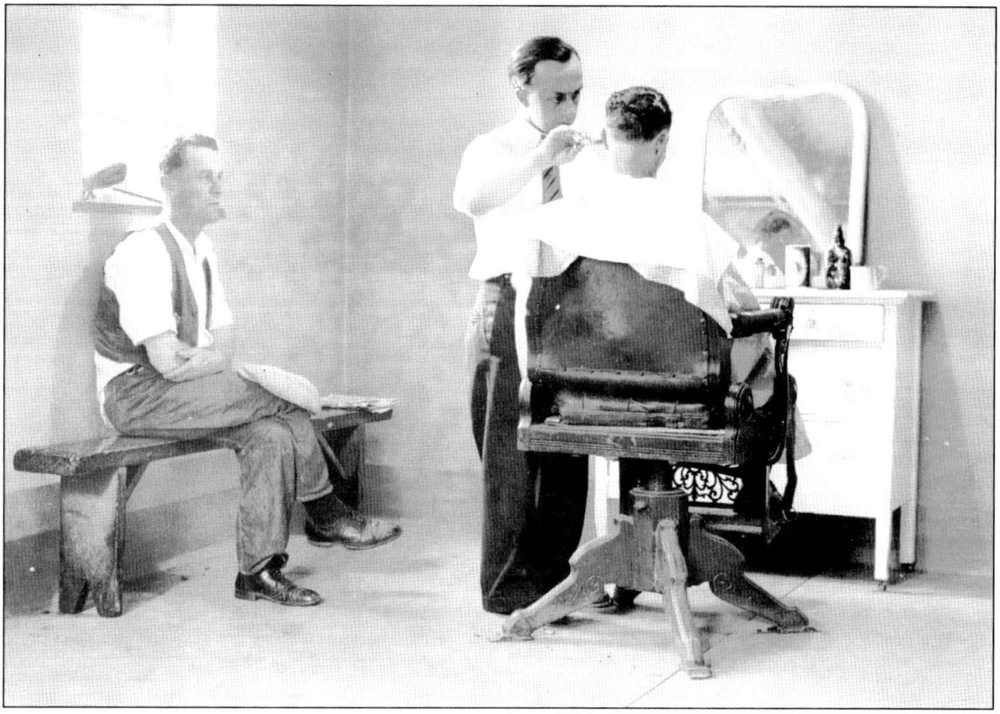

Pictured in 1934 are three residents of Camp Greycourt giving and receiving haircuts. Most of the men at the camp worked on the farm, but some cut hair, cooked, and worked as custodians.

The residents of Camp Greycourt are shown in 1934 resting in the shade and taking a break from farming the fields.

Residents of Camp Greycourt dig up slate and make a stone wall to line the entrance to the main building in 1934.

Pictured in 1934 is the staff of Camp Greycourt. Joseph A. Mannix, superintendent of the Municipal Lodging House, is on the far left, and his wife, Ann Mannix, is on the far right. They are seated on the front steps of the camp's main building.

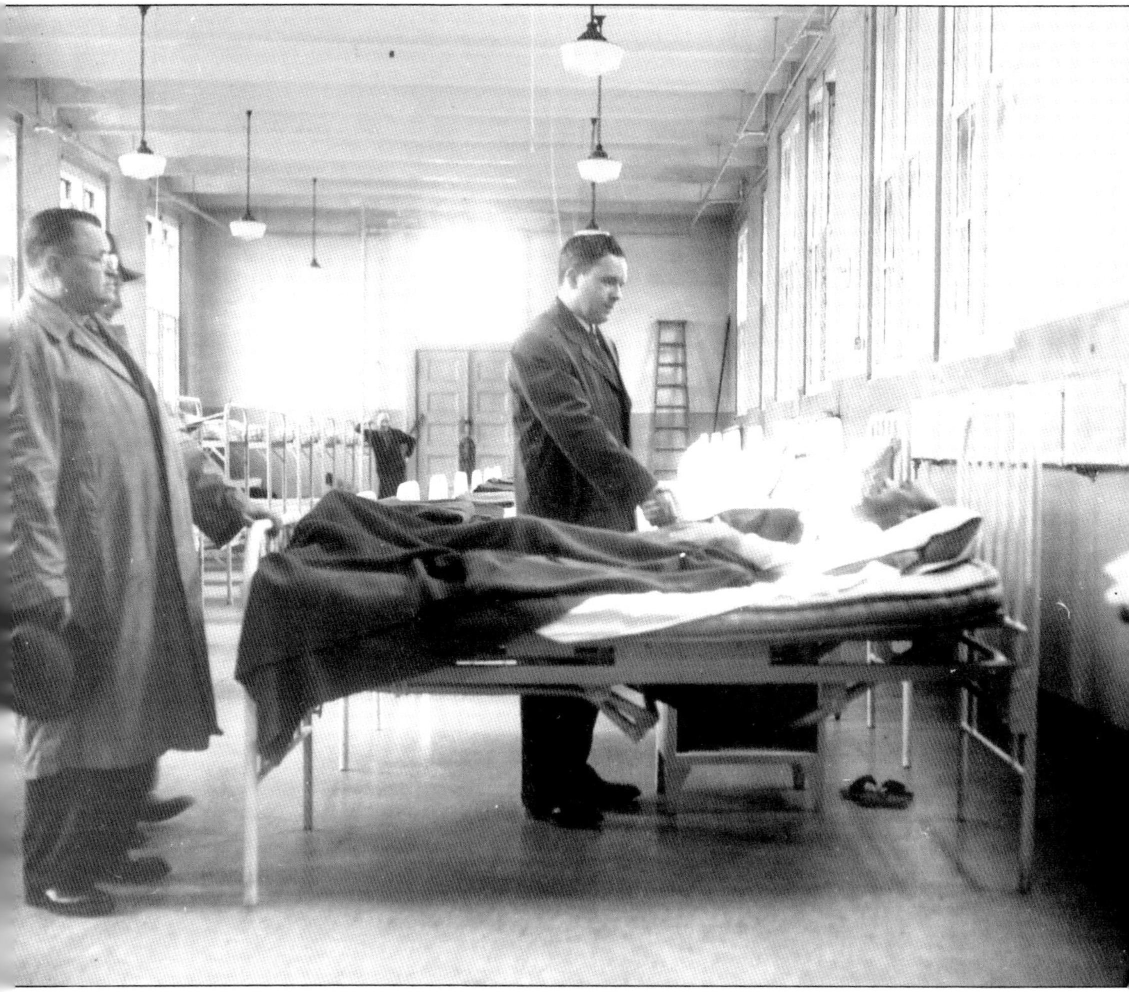

Joseph A. Mannix, director of the Hart Island rehabilitation center for homeless men, is pictured on March 23, 1953. Also in the picture is Judge Mustagh shaking hands with one of the residents of Hart Island. Hart Island was used as a rehabilitation home for 2,000 homeless men in 1950.